EMPOWER YOURSELF

Know the system, Know your rights, Know what to do!

Insurance companies are in the business to make money from premiums and to keep claim costs at a minimum. They are experienced professionals who know all the angles to protect their own interests. You hired them to be allies in the event of a disaster but you may end up being treated as an adversary when you submit a claim. Don't be one of the thousands of homeowners who will be short-changed this year because they don't know the system and how to make it work for them. *Top Dollar Property Claims* tells you everything you need to know (in language that's easy to understand) for you to get the best property insurance settlement possible.

Learn the secrets of successful top dollar settlements!

- documenting your claim
- building a file that works for you
- dealing with the troublesome adjuster
- using line itemization to substantiate the damage estimate
- using laws and regulations to negotiate your claim
- using the right pricing guides to accurately determine the claim's value

BONUS - get dozens of sample letters and forms that will make your claims process easier and save you hundreds of dollars!

Your legitimate claim deserves a positive response from your insurance company. The following testimonials are actual results others have achieved by using the valuable information contained in this book.

"My insurance company wanted to settle my claim for only $740. By following the techniques and suggestions contained in **Top Dollar Property Claims,** *my claim was settled for more than $31,000!" I highly recommend every homeowner have a copy of this book.*

Nella McNamara - Homeowner

"A local church had a major roof leak and the water stained the open beam ceilings and carpets. The insurance company tried to settle the claim for $1,800, but because I utilized the information contained in **Top Dollar Property Claims,** *we settled for over $235,000!"*

Robert Tuffnell - Contractor

"My insurance adjuster was non-responsive to my calls and it was taking forever to settle my claim. Once **Top Dollar Property Claims** *showed me how to get his attention, the adjuster was eager to settle my claim."*

Cindy Ritter. - Homeowner

"My insurance company denied my water damage claim. After reading **Top Dollar Property Claims**, *I contacted the Insurance Commissioner's office and they got involved. By the time we were done, my insurance company paid the entire claim."*

Dennis M. - Homeowner

"Don't settle your property insurance claim until you read Top Dollar Property Claims!"
Ted Hopton - Insurance Claims Litigator

TOP DOLLAR PROPERTY CLAIMS

SECRETS TO SUCCESSFUL
INSURANCE CLAIM SETTLEMENTS

Les Watrous
Orange, California - U.S.A.

TGWB Publishing, Inc.

Publisher's Cataloging-in-Publication
(Provided by Quality Books, Inc)

Watrous, Les
  Top dollar property claims : secrets to successful insurance claims settlements / Les Watrous, - 1st ed.
  p. cm.
  Includes bibliographical references and index.
  ISBN: 0-9654537-1-5

  1. Homeowners' insurance--Handbooks, manuals, etc. 2. Insurance--Adjustment of claims--Handbooks, manuals, etc. 3. Property insurance--Handbooks, manuals, etc. 4. Insurance claims--Handbooks, manuals, etc. I. Title.

  HG9986.W38 1998   **368.1**
                                           QBI97-41025

TGWB Publishing, Inc.
2232 E. Wilson Avenue
Orange, CA 92867
(714) 744-6750

10 9 8 7 6 5 4 3 2 1   ISBN 0-9654537-1-5

Sources & Acknowledgements

Many thanks to all who contributed to the information contained in this book.
Contributors include: insurance associations, departments of insurance, insurance companies, contractors, engineers, senior
claims adjusters and attorneys. A special thanks to those who worked directly on this book: Ted Hopton, Ron Wilson, Elaine
Watrous, Gordon Carle, Shawna Frenzel, Jim Herman, John Keyes and the Law Offices of Philip L. Hummel, IV.
The writers, editors, proofreaders and illustrators are much appreciated for their dedication and commitment to this project.
If it were not for their help, this book would not have been possible.
Les Watrous - Author

National Association of Insurance Commissioners
International Conference of Building Officials
Federal Emergency Management Administration (FEMA)
Independent Insurance Agent & Brokers Association
Small Business Administration (SBA)
Registry of Insurance Repair Professionals™
National Insurance Institute
Insurance Information Institute
The National Underwriter Co.
Insurance Services Office
California Department of Insurance
Florida Department of Insurance
New York Department of Insurance
AAA Insurance
Aetna Insurance
Allstate Insurance
Amica Insurance
Farmers Insurance
Firemans Fund
State Farm Insurance
USAA Insurance
20th Century Insurance

In writing this book, we want to make it absolutely clear that the majority of individuals, be they homeowners, contractors, or insurance personnel, are fair minded and dedicated people. Just as in life itself, there will be many types of people and personalities meeting one another in cooperation or confrontation during the insurance claims process. Unfortunately, there are unscrupulous contractors, opportunistic homeowners and troublesome claims adjusters. We make mention of the fact that you may meet these types of individuals along the road during your insurance claim process, but we also stress the point that the majority of the people you will encounter will be compassionate and empathetic to your situation and experience.

<u>*References To Keep Handy*</u>

National Association of Insurance Commissioners

12 Wyandotte Plaza
120 W. 12th St., Suite 1100
Kansas City, Mo. 64105
(816) 842-3600

Founded in 1871, The NAIC is the organization of insurance regulators for the 50 states, the District of Columbia, and the four U.S. territories. The NAIC provides a forum for the development of uniform public policy when uniformity is appropriate.

A state regulator's primary responsibility is to protect the interests of insurance consumers, and the NAIC helps regulators fulfill that obligation. That assistance is related to the regulator's shared objectives of financial and market conduct regulation. For assistance in contacting your state's insurance commissioner or other publications about the insurance industry, contact the NAIC at 816-374-7259.

Insurance Information Institute

110 Williams Street, 4th Floor
New York, NY 10038
(212) 669-9200 or (800) 942-4242
Online: www.iii.org

Insurance Information Institute is a non-profit, educational and communications organization sponsored by the auto, home and business insurance industry. This is an information center for insurance related publications, abstracts, statistics, facts and figures. Online services include catalogs of publications available to the public as well as consumer alerts and answers to your insurance related questions via the E-mail address consumer@iii.org

National Insurance Consumers Helpline

(800) 942-4242 from 8:00 a.m. to 8:00p.m.,
EST, Monday through Friday.

This consumer orientated helpline is dedicated to educating consumers about what insurance is and how it works. This helpline informs consumers of the latest developments in the insurance marketplace and insurance tips. It also offers brochures and catalogs covering a wide variety of insurance related information. The helpline is provided by Insurance Information Institute.

National Consumer's League

1701 K Street, N.W., Suite 1201
Washington, D.C. 20006
Telephone: (202) 835-3323
Fax: (202) 835-0747
Online: http://www.natlconsumersleague.org

The mission of the National Consumers League is to identify, protect, represent, and advance the economic and social interests of consumers and workers. The National Consumers League is a private, nonprofit advocacy group representing consumers on marketplace and workplace issues. They are the nation's oldest consumer organization.

Registry of Insurance Repair Professionals™

A national internet database directory of professionals that specializes in the insurance restoration industry. Listings in the registry range from material suppliers, restoration contractors, structural, mechanical and soils engineers, architects, appraisers, and attorneys to the various tradesmen that specialize in facilitating insurance repairs. (For more information about the registry see page 158)

http:\\www.repair-registry.com

FORWARD

Your home is probably the most important investment you will make. It protects your family and your belongings, and you count on its appreciating value for your future. Maintaining its value is probably one of your utmost concerns. When an event occurs that causes you to suffer a loss to your property, it sets you back emotionally, as well as financially. Your deepest wish is that the incident had never occurred. You wish that your home was in the condition it was in prior to your loss.

If you purchased full replacement insurance, **that's exactly what you are entitled to!**

YOU ARE ENTITLED TO HAVE YOUR PROPERTY RESTORED TO THE SAME CONDITION IT WAS IN BEFORE IT WAS DAMAGED

We hope and pray that all is safe and sound and we want to express our empathy to you for having to deal with any kind of a property loss. Losses, small or large, can be very traumatic experiences and can generate a great deal of frustration and stress.

Although there are many kinds of losses that are suffered, the purpose of this book is directed to property losses. It is our hope that we can help relieve some of the confusion and anxiety that comes with having to restore your property. This step-by-step guide is what you need to get your property restored to the same condition it was in before the incident occurred. It will show you how to get a *"Top Dollar Property Claim."*

We wish you the very best!

SHOULD YOU FILE A CLAIM?

**"Three out of five Americans with property insurance file
at least one insurance claim during their lifetime."**
—*Kiplingers Personal Finance Magazine*

Utilizing the protection of your homeowners insurance policy can be a daunting proposition. The reluctance to "file a claim" is a consideration we all make with preconceived ideas that a submitted claim will increase premium rates or even cause cancellation. This sort of thinking was created in the building boom of the 50's, perpetuated in the 60's, reaffirmed in the 70's, challenged in the 80's, and is being discounted in the 90's!

The following statistics illustrate the growing trend for homeowners to employ their existing policies and overcome the reluctance to file a claim to which they are entitled. These statistics are based on reported claims, and do not reflect claims that homeowners have not filed, for a variety of reasons, and losses that fell below the deductible amount of their policies.

Statistical source: Insurance Information Institute, U.S.A., Abstract of Insurance Statistics.

- **Total of all property and fire claims filed in last year — over 22,850,000 (22.85 million). On average, that's about 1 out of every 5 households each year!**

- **Claims payout in dollars — over $7,957,000,000 (7.957 billion dollars)**

- **Nationwide (50 states) average claims submission — 62,602 claims per day**

TABLE OF CONTENTS

CHAPTER 11

CHAPTER 12

CHAPTER 13

CHAPTER 14

CHAPTER 15

CHAPTER 16

Read the entire book! It has good information !

CHAPTER 1

DISASTER! WHAT TO DO?
A S.I.M.P.L.E. GUIDE™

SAFETY FIRST

INVESTIGATE DAMAGES

MITIGATE DAMAGES

PHOTOGRAPH DAMAGES

LIST DAMAGES

EMERGENCY SERVICES

SAFETY FIRST

Above all else, you, your family and other loved ones are the primary concern in any emergency. The key words and response in any emergency are DON'T PANIC! The paramount concern is to get everyone out of harm's way.

Assuming that your family is safe from the immediate emergency, let's now consider the overall sphere of safety and how it can quickly turn into a liability nightmare for you, the homeowner.

If you have sustained damage to a broken pipe, there may be a toxic hazard issue to consider. Sewage that backs up and floods to neighboring properties, broken pipes encased in walls, plumbing that shifts and breaks during earth movement can be a bio-health problem.

If you are a victim of wind and/or rain damage, you may have portions of roofing or dwelling structure creating an unsafe condition to the general public. This can be a major hazard and leaves you open to liability exposure.

Broken glass from windows, or trees that have damaged structural supports, can cause you one big headache, and will intensify the unsafe condition of your home, unless you take action.

If you are equipped to deal with the problem, you must stem the flow of broken pipes, board up broken windows, cover exposed roofing tiles, strengthen structural supports which have weakened, and post proper warning signs (no trespass, etc...) or barricades if the damage poses a danger to the public.

Keeping your family and the public away from exposed danger is too often overlooked. Remember, broken pipes cause flooding and flooding can cause surfaces, indoors and outdoors, to be extremely slippery and may cause an accident.

Insurance claims are generally based on the doctrine of proximate cause. Proximate cause essentially means "something must happen which is the direct cause of the damage."

If something or someone intervenes in the flow from cause to damage, and that intervening force is a negligent act, then the liability for the escalation of damage may be deemed to be the responsibility of the intervenor. In other words, don't make the problem worse by inaction or negligence.

Your intervening act can be your good intentions to secure the premises and the dangerous condition, but can also lead to a denied claim by your insurance company if you are negligent in performing that act. Conversely, if you fail to act in a timely manner to mitigate your damages, you may be held responsible for further damage.

In other words, if the damage to a broken pipe causes water to flood your walkway, and you fail to mitigate the damage by not turning the water flow off within the first few minutes, you may be jeopardizing part of your claim if your neighbor rushes over to assist you, slips on the wet sidewalk and injures himself.

Time is obviously a factor. If you failed to attempt to shut off the water flow since the breakage, and several hours has elapsed when your neighbor is injured, an insurance company may take the position that you were negligent as an intervening force, and that the initial broken pipe damage was not the proximate cause of your neighbor's injury. The cost to resolve your neighbor's claim could come directly out of your pocket.

Your responsibility to make the premises safe should be a prime concern as the homeowner.

One area that should be approached with extreme caution is the broken gas pipe. If you find yourself in this situation, the first thing you should do is evacuate everyone in the house. If you can locate the gas meter outside of the dwelling, use a proper tool (crescent wrench) to turn the gas valve to the closed position and immediately contact the gas company for assistance.

Another example would be if a strong wind was blowing roof debris around your neighborhood and you attempted to cover the roof area with insufficient sheeting. If a passerby, one block away, was struck by a loose shingle and injured, your attempt to prevent further damage (even though honorable) could come

under close scrutiny by your insurance company's investigation and evaluation of your claim.

One thing should be mentioned at this time, and that is to never, ever put yourself or anyone else in jeopardy of injury while securing a damaged dwelling.

It is best sometimes to call upon a company that can handle emergency services (i.e., plumber, electrician, deflooding experts, restoration contractor, etc.) in order to quickly and efficiently minimize the exposed danger and to help reduce you from further liability.

INVESTIGATE DAMAGES

If your first assessment is that of severe damage, leave the premises immediately. Your first reaction to  the severity of the damage is usually right. Don't jeopardize your safety or that of your family. A large branch of a tree crashing down upon your roof can damage the internal components and structural support of the entire house. It is best to leave the house and go to a neighbor's home or hotel until you can properly assess the damage.

It is also wise, at this time, to consider calling in a qualified restoration contractor* or specific emergency service. Your choice is simple, either you and your family combat the disaster, such as a broken pipe or leaking roof, or you call in the experts.

A restoration contractor or an emergency service company can shut off water flow, cover the roof, extract flooded areas of your home (deflooding), dry or remove wet carpeting, move furniture out of harm's way, and more! They can also secure your home or business to prevent vandalism, trespassing, or any other condition that may hold you vulnerable to liability or affect the safety of others.

* see Chapter 13

KEEP A CRESCENT WRENCH IN BOTH YOUR GAS AND WATER METER BOX FOR QUICK ACCESS DURING AN EMERGENCY.

MITIGATE DAMAGES

To mitigate, according to Webster's New World Dictionary, means to "make less severe, less painful." To mitigate damages, in insurance jargon, is to use reasonable efforts to lessen the damages which have already occurred. Every insurance policy contains the express condition that the policyholder, upon suffering a loss, prevent further damage and to "mitigate" the situation.

Generally speaking, your response to a loss will depend on the type of loss and the circumstances surrounding it.

Broken Water Pipe: This occurrence can happen at anytime. It doesn't matter whether your home is old or new, piping within the structure can be a problem. Broken pipes can cause immediate flooding, damaging the contents and interior of your home.

Older homes utilizing galvanized plumbing components can age and deteriorate to the point that one day a rupture occurs. Newer homes can have inadequately installed plumbing and piping which can cause leaks and pressure build-up resulting in fracture and flood.

When a broken pipe occurs, quickly assess the damage. Your primary response should be to turn off the main valve controlling the water flow into your house. A further step that should be taken to "mitigate" your damages in this case would be to mop up all exposed water and extract any water out of the carpeting to prevent further damage and avoid deterioration.

You should be prepared, in advance, to locate the water shutoff valve, and inform other members of your household how and where to turn off the water.

There are a number of ways to curtail the flow of water to your residence.

1) Valve nearest to the source of the broken pipe;

2) Main input valve to residence; and

3) Municipal shutoff valve at curbside.

Have the right shutoff tool handy.

Most under sink and toilet shutoff valves have the common spindle-wheel type valve closure handle. But others, such as your main-to-house or municipal (the one located in your parkway or metered water box on street facing) water shutoffs have slot-turn valves.

A medium size adjustable crescent wrench will be the best preparation you can have in case of an emergency of this sort. If a pipe breaks, for example, under a sink or toilet, the valve nearest to the break is probably the appropriate shutoff. Under each sink in your home is either a two-valve (hot and cold water) assembly or, in the case of a toilet, a one-valve shutoff.

SHUT VALVES OFF IMMEDIATELY BY TURNING IN A CLOCKWISE MOTION

Sometimes valves can be hard to rotate due to calcium build-up from the water, but a little effort back and forth can loosen and free them up enough to allow you to close the water flow in a clockwise direction. It is also a good idea to periodically maintain the efficiency of the shutoff valve by spraying a threading lubricant, such as the commercially available WD-40, at the valve stem.

Pipe break occurrences normally involve under sink piping and fixtures, kitchen pipes and garbage disposal in-flows, and hot water heating units. Pipes can also break within a wall, floor or ceiling. If this is the case, and there is no valve located near the break, you must then shut off water flow to the entire house.

Home and Municipal Water Shutoff

The main input valve to your home is normally located at the front or side of your house. You will locate this spindle-wheel valve close to the ground or possibly in shallow dirt directly below ground level. Again, a clockwise turn will shut this valve off completely, stopping all water flow to the household.

The municipal water shutoff, or the valve that comes from your city's supply to your house, is normally located at the site of the water meter. Most urban areas have this valve and meter box located on the "parkway" or that portion of your property at the city boundary located at a street site. It is the location where city officials and meter readers periodically check and account for your water use.

A medium-sized crescent wrench can be used to de-activate water flow, but if you have difficulty in closing the valve, call your city's water emergency service immediately.

PHOTOGRAPH DAMAGES

The best way, by far, to document any loss for insurance claim purposes is to photograph or videotape the damages.

It is vitally important that you obtain well lit photographs/videos of the damaged areas.

Water damage may dry quickly, and if there is no confirmable evidence of the interior stains to your ceiling or walls, they could go undetected. Flooded areas subside eventually, and the power of a detailed photograph/video showing the immediate disaster may enhance your insurance claim immensely.

Always request double prints when you get your film developed and keep the negatives in a safe place. This way you will have one set for your file and another set can be sent to the insurance company.

LIST DAMAGES (INVENTORY)

The sooner you can list or inventory the loss, the better.

At the time of the loss you are more aware of what has been damaged and the cause of such damage. There are items or components that you may miss after a day or two of contemplating your loss.

Photographs are indeed the best evidence in any insurance claim, but a detailed inventory of damaged or destroyed property will eventually become invaluable in processing your claim. Perhaps you already have photos or video tape of your home to show the "before" condition of your home.

EMERGENCY SERVICES

Homeowners need immediate assistance and damage assessment when they experience an insurance loss. You also want a plan of action on the repairs that will have to be made, and where you will go during the repair period if your home is uninhabitable.

If you have experienced a broken pipe and you need assistance, immediately call a plumber. Water damage (flooding) should be handled by a water extraction (deflooding) service. Wind damage can be repaired by a roofing contractor. These service companies can be easily located in your local telephone yellow pages. Be

sure to ask these companies if they qualify to work with insurance companies, and what their experience is in doing so.

You must remember that most of these service companies demand payment immediately. This means that the money is coming out of your pocket before you can submit a claim to your insurance company. In other words, you are subsidizing your insurance carrier, wherein it should be the other way around. In a majority of cases the insurance company should be paying for your emergency expenses immediately.

You may also be inclined to contact a general contractor to repair or rebuild your loss. There are a number of differences between a general contractor and a restoration contractor. These differences are discussed in detail in Chapter 13 "Hiring The Right Contractor(s)."

You may also be approached by what is known as a public adjuster. Beware!

Public adjusters are independents who generate their income by charging you, the homeowner, to adjust your claim. They are often aggressive disaster marketeers, determined to arrive at your catastrophe even before emergency units arrive. They may charge you anywhere from 15% to 50% (or more) of your claim, depending on the total amount. This means you will have to make up the difference personally to pay for their "services." You may be losing in two ways: First, you will be paying a percentage for someone to handle your claim, which you could do yourself. Second, because you have already paid exorbitant fees to an adjuster, the reliability and professionalism of any contractor you hire will be limited due to the decreased amount of funds remaining to complete the work.

According to the general manager of Economy Restorations™, a full-service restoration company in Orange, California: "Qualified restoration contractors can save homeowners enormous amounts of time and money by acting as a liaison between the insurance company and the homeowner. They can also be the saving grace of a homeowner in distress—on the scene quickly to provide an emergency crew to secure the residence and make immediate repairs in order to avoid increasing the damage potential. Restoration contractors provide services such as board-up of windows and doors, temporary roof coverings and, if necessary, secure the structure with steel beams. Furniture, carpet and upholstery may also be removed and emergency electricity added to provide temporary power if the occupants are to remain in the house during restoration."

Even before the homeowner's own insurance company is on the scene, the restoration contractor and his/her representatives can quell the anxieties of the homeowner and begin the initial stages of recovery of the property.

A qualified restoration contracting firm can handle the devastating loss experienced by the homeowner no matter what the degree of damage. They can make life easier for the homeowner by bringing in the professionals that are needed to restore the house. The restoration contractor can arrange for painters, roofers, carpenters and other specialists to perform work on the damaged house. Restoration contractors will also coordinate any additional subcontractors for the work to be done, and make sure that the people doing the subcontracted work are licensed, bonded and insured, and will effectuate the repair of your home promptly.

Respected restoration companies usually look out for the best interest of all, including the insurance company, and should be truthful in assessing the damaged items and replacement value needed.

CHAPTER 2
YOU'VE HAD A LOSS . . . NOW WHAT?

- **START A FILE NOW!**
- **CLAIMANT'S RESPONSIBILITIES**
- **EVALUATE YOUR LOSS**
- **ADDITIONAL PHOTOGRAPHS**

- **SHOULD YOU FILE A CLAIM?**
- **GATHER INFORMATION**
- **SHOULD YOU CALL YOUR AGENT?**
- **DO YOU REALLY NEED THREE BIDS?**

A tree crashed through your living room. The wind blew shingles off your roof.
A fire burned your kitchen. A broken pipe flooded your house.

Remember, you normally have up to 60 days to file a claim for damages but be sure to review your own policy. Do not hurry to file a claim if you are not fully prepared. One day or two will not always typically enhance your claim, nor motivate your insurance company or assigned adjuster to be more generous or expedite your claim any faster. If you file your claim too soon, you may be overlooking damage related to the cause that may be discovered after you have settled and signed a release with your insurance company.

START A FILE NOW !

You should start a file on your loss immediately and keep it properly maintained until your loss has been completely satisfied and you have received all the lien releases and warranties from contractors.

Your attitude in starting and keeping your file accurate should be one of preparation in case you need to defend yourself or to preserve your legal rights. Remember, the insurance company is keeping a file on you!

WHAT YOUR FILE SHOULD HAVE

- **A Current Copy of Your Insurance Policy**
- **Copies of Written Communications**
- **A Telephone - FAX Log**

The telephone-fax log might seem like extraneous work to maintain during the claim processing phase, but it can prove to be invaluable when it comes to reciting your position, and may have an impact on the kind of service you receive from the claims office.

By keeping the telephone-fax log active, you establish a clear record of the times you called your adjuster and the times he or she may have failed to return your call. It will also verify faxes sent by you

---

There are forms in Chapter 16 for you to use or modify
depending on the nature of your claim.

to your adjuster. Be sure to retain your fax machine's verification of "pages sent" on the date of transmission.

Document Everything!

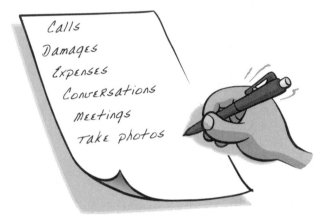

Calls
Damages
Expenses
Conversations
Meetings
Take photos

• A Claims Processing Information Checklist

If you follow the Claims Processing Checklist, you will be taking a giant step in the right direction in minimizing any obstacles or hassles that may arise during the claims processing period.

The checklist is self-explanatory so it shouldn't cause you any anxiety or confusion when you are preparing your claim (see Chapter 16).

Follow all of the requirements of the checklist. If you bypass a checkpoint, expect to see your adjuster pounce on that one item which you may have overlooked.

• An Expense Log

Your expense log will put money back into your pocket. If you have to pay for emergency services (plumber, electrician, etc.) or for living expenses in advance, your expense log will confirm that payment. Your receipt for those services will validate those payments. Be sure you record all expenses, no matter how insignificant they may seem. You are establishing a record of what the claim is costing you, not only in money, but in time. Your adjuster may be impressed by your concise recordkeeping,

and should consider your total expenses as part and parcel of the claim.

• A Receipt Envelope

Keep all original receipts. If the insurance company wants receipts, give them copies.

The receipt envelope is as important as your expense log. This will validate your expense log entries. A simple 8 1/2" x 11" envelope attached inside your insurance file can  function as a depository of all receipts for items or services regarding your loss during the entire claims processing period.

The saddest sound that you have ever heard is your sigh when the adjuster says, "If only you had a receipt, I would have paid on it."

• A Loss Summary

The summary of your loss should be a brief description of your insurance loss and the resultant damages you intend to claim. Be as accurate as possible but also know that in the event of a lawsuit, any information in writing may be obtained in a court of law as evidence. Contemporaneous observation (existing or occurring during the same time) is always your best source of recollection. The purpose of a loss summary is for you to put down any initial impressions of your loss. This information can be used to help create and maintain your file as well as to provide a quick reference of your loss and any pertinent information, in case you need to arbitrate or litigate your claim.

Ask yourself:

Who?

Who has sustained the loss? Does the claimant have an insurable interest in the property? Whose name appears on the policy?

What?

What was specifically damaged? Inventory? Were the contents (furniture/personal property) of your home affected? Was the ceiling fan in your living room, bedroom, or kitchen shorted-out by water damage? Will it have to be removed in the restoration of your home? What electrical outlets appear to be inoperable as a result of damage?

Where?

Where did your loss occur? List the complete address, including county and zip code. In what area of the house? List the rooms where damage occurred. Draw a diagram of walls, ceilings, doors and windows where the damage occurred.

When?

When did the loss occur? What time? AM? PM? Weekend or weekday? Month, day, year?

How?

How did the loss occur? If it was roof damage caused by wind and rain, were shingles blown away? Did rain seep into the interior of your home? How were the living room, bedroom and den affected when the ceilings and walls began to crack and leak?

• Copy of Proof of Loss

When you have completed your Proof of Loss form (see Chapter 16), keep a copy in your file for reference.

• A List of Damaged Structure and Personal Property Photo List

Make a list of any and all damaged areas, including personal property and take corresponding photos which will show the particulars.

• Photos

Take a lot of photos and get them developed right away. Examine the photos for clarity of what they are supposed to show. If they are not clear or don't show what you wanted, take more photos and get close-ups. Especially look to see if water stains show up. Get double prints when you develop the photos and save the negatives. One set will go to the insurance company and one set will go in your file. It would also be helpful if you can send copies of photographs or video which show the original condition of your property before the loss.

• Progress Photos

If possible, take photos throughout the work progress to show the different stages of construction.

• Photo Sheet(s)

The photo sheet(s) can be the most important bit of evidence you possess in your claim file. It is imperative that you retain originals of all the photographs or video tapes you have sent to the adjuster. Photographs and videos are too easily "lost" in file transfer or misdirected mail.

Your photographs and videos are what is known in legal circles as "best evidence," which may have more impact in the courts of law than eyewitnesses.

• A Chronology of Events

Always document when you receive any correspondence, compare the correspondence date to the postal date and <u>always</u> save the envelope.

Always document when anyone comes out to look at your damages, including contractors, engineers and repairmen. Document what they looked at and what comments they may have made regarding your loss.

Always document when the insurance adjuster comes out, specifically what the adjuster did and looked at, and state if it appeared to you that the adjuster handled your claim professionally and thoroughly.

• 10-Point Claims Submission

The 10-Point Claims Submission form is another very important checklist (see Chapter 16). Do not omit any of the checklist items. Remember to send copies of documents and evidence. One important note: Send all correspondence via certified mail, return receipt requested. It may be a bit more costly, but you will never find yourself in the situation where the assigned adjuster just happens to "not have received your letter."

Like in any high profile industry, the insurance claims offices are not immune to overzealous and "low loss-ratio" minded individuals acting in the capacity of adjusters. Not receiving your letter or fax can be a deceptive way of stalling or delaying the final outcome of your claim. Some are empathetic to your cause and want to see your file closed as soon as possible. Be aware of the adjuster who may lack people skills and has "missed the boat" when his/her training manual calls for quality customer service.

Lastly, keep in mind that your organizational skills in creating and maintaining a claims file will enhance your ability to process your claim smoothly and will provide the added power of preparation.

Attempting to recreate a file, late in a claims processing undertaking, is virtually impossible.

- **Keep Copies of all Professional Reports**

- **Keep Repair Estimates or Scope of Repairs**

- **Keep Copies of all Contracts, Work Orders and Additional Work / Change Orders**

- **Keep a Workers List**

  Maintain a list of everyone who works on your home, who they work for and what they are doing. It sometimes even helps to take their photo as they are working.

- **Lien Releases**

  Always get unconditional lien releases from all workers before you make any payments.

- **Get all City and County Building Code Requirements in Writing**

CLAIMANT'S RESPONSIBILITIES

According to the standard homeowner policy, certain actions are required of the policyholder. If you have reviewed your policy, you will probably be awestruck by the small, fine print indicating declarations of time of loss, location of loss, etc. that you must provide. Don't be dismayed as these requirements generally boil down to the four listed below.

The insured shall:

1) give immediate written notice (proof of loss form) to the insurance company of any loss;

2) protect the property from further damage;

3) forthwith separate the damaged and undamaged property, and put it in the best possible order;

4) furnish a complete inventory of the destroyed and/or damaged property, showing in detail the quantities, costs, value and the amount of loss claimed.

The insurance policy interpretation of "immediate" generally means within a reasonable time. Most policies usually allow for a period of up to 60 days, upon the discovery of the damaged property, to file a claim.

BE SURE TO CHECK YOUR OWN STATE'S STATUTE OF LIMITATIONS AND THE LIMITS OF YOUR OWN POLICY!

EVALUATE YOUR LOSS

Make a list of everything damaged, including:

- A detailed description of each item, the date of purchase, and what it would cost to replace it (if you have replacement-cost coverage).

- Any relevant receipts, bills, photographs, or serial numbers from appliances and electronic equipment will help establish the value of your losses. The adjuster may want to see all damaged items, so avoid throwing out anything.

- Take photographs or videos of any damage to your house or other buildings on the property.

Keep careful records. Make copies of all information you give your insurer in connection with your claim. Be sure to hold onto everything the insurer gives you. It's also a good idea to take notes of all meetings and conversations you have with your agent, insurer and/or claims adjuster.

- Make a list of everything you want to show the adjuster, from cracks in the walls to missing roof tiles.

- Don't make permanent repairs before consulting with your agent or claims adjuster, unless absolutely necessary or to mitigate damages.

ADDITIONAL PHOTOGRAPHS

It cannot be overemphasized that the more photographs/videos you take, the better the outcome of your claim. Wind and water damage can be altered by nature and drying. Loose roof shingles can blow back into place concealing underlying damage and you might be unable to photograph the evidence if taken a day or a week after your loss. The same goes for water damage. Discoloration on walls and ceilings can disappear through drying, and appear to have no damage, when the internal water damage has weakened and damaged the wall or ceiling. Electrical shorts can result as a product of water damage, so smoke or discoloration around switches and outlets is very important to photograph. A good idea is to have another person in the photograph/video pointing out the damaged area. Check your lighting. Poor lighting can sometimes hide the true nature of the damage. You can also take the photos/videos with a ruler in the frame as a reference or date your photos with the front page of a newspaper in your pictures.

SHOULD YOU FILE A CLAIM?

If you have suffered a valid loss, by all means, file a claim with your insurance carrier.

Some homeowners are reluctant to file, no matter how big of a loss their home has sustained. A lot of this hesitant attitude comes from the often recited tale that if you file, you will be cancelled. If you follow that type of reasoning, then you should be asking yourself, "why over a working lifetime (calculated as 40 years) will I have contributed, by way of premiums, a total of over $62,000.00 to my insurance carrier?" This is money you are paying to the insurance company for protection from a loss. Why would you ever be shy about filing a claim?

If you happen to be one of those homeowners that bad luck seems to follow and you unfortunately have more than a couple of claims a year, this may cause concern to the insurance company and they may view you as a multiple claimant.

The insurance company industry will never admit to the idea that they selectively review or "red line" neighborhoods for policy cancellation and underwriter reviews. But they do.

The insurance companies usually give the following list of reasons why rates vary. You will notice that not once are the words "claims" or "multiple claims" mentioned.

1) LOCATION: Companies keep records of the claims they've had to pay, dividing territory by cities, zip codes and even neighborhoods, to determine the risk of insuring homes. Residents of areas with traditionally high losses from crimes, fires, or natural disasters can expect to pay more than residents of low loss areas.

2) FIRE-PROTECTION CLASS: How close is your home to the nearest fire station? How well-trained are the firefighters? The closer you are to a fire station and the better the firefighters are, the lower your premiums should be. The Insurance Services Office, an industry advisory organization, assigns every neighborhood in the U.S. a fire-protection class, based on the quality of fire protection and the distance of homes from a water source (some large insurance companies use their own rating systems). For that reason, a rural home miles from a fire station may cost more to insure than an urban home in a higher-crime area located around the corner from a firehouse.

3) TYPE OF BUILDING: Wooden houses generally cost more to insure than brick houses because brick houses withstand fire and natural damage better. Earthquake insurance, however, costs considerably less for wooden houses because they withstand quakes better than brick houses.

4) AGE OF HOME: Companies may charge up to 20 percent less to insure new homes than to insure older ones, because older homes may be more susceptible to damage in storms and fires. Outdated building standards and old wiring can also make older homes riskier to insure.

YOUR POLICY DOES <u>NOT</u> REQUIRE YOU TO HAVE THREE BIDS !!!

5) CONSTRUCTION COSTS: The cost for building materials and labor vary greatly from one part of the country to another. The more it would cost the insurer to repair or rebuild your home, the higher your premium is likely to be.

6) NUMBER OF UNITS: Companies may charge more to insure apartments or condominiums in large buildings than in small buildings because the risk of fire and other damage and loss increases with the number of occupants. The risk increases proportionately with the number of occupants of any dwelling.

Insurance companies are in business to stay in business. In other words, insurance is not protection sold to you, rather, it is an investment of the money you give to insurance companies as premiums. These investments are how insurance companies make a profit. So it really boils down to a numbers game.

When the insurance company receives a claim, they set up what is known as "reserves." These reserves are in accordance with the insurance laws governing the industry and is the money put aside to pay claims. Simply stated, while you are waiting for a settlement, they are investing the money put aside to pay you.

If you file a claim, the reserve amount (or the amount they anticipate paying) is calculated against your time as an insured, your premium payment, your risk factor of reoccurring claims and the age of your policy.

If you file multiple claims, you can surmise what this does to the insurance evaluation of you as a risk. Is it better to pay your claim and drop you as an insured? Or is it better to pay your claim and increase your premiums?

When individuals shout, "I'm going to sue my insurance company for raising my rates," remember you, and you alone, will be taking on the big boys. Incidentally, just three of the nation's biggest insurance companies net assets in 1995 were in excess of $231 billion dollars!

GATHER INFORMATION

Find your policy. Your homeowners insurance policy should be easily accessible. You should have a copy of your policy secured in a safe place away from the residence, such as in a safe deposit box, at your office, or at your attorney's office. You should, of course, have a copy of the policy readily available in your home to review and update your coverage and to determine any exclusions to your claim.

Section "D" (Coverage - D) of a standard homeowners policy allows for temporary living expenses and expenses to cover immediate repairs. Check your policy to confirm your coverage of these items carefully.

Remember, with the exception of restoration contractors, most repair persons will demand payment immediately, whereas the restoration contractor should wait for payment from the insurance company to be compensated for the work performed.

Also, be sure to check the amount of your deductible. This is the amount that you must pay to the insurance company before your claim can be paid.

SHOULD YOU CALL YOUR AGENT?

Your agent can give you invaluable information and direction to follow after suffering a loss. Your agent is aware of the coverages contained in your policy and can give immediate feedback as to the coverage of your claim. Your agent can also be a friend who you should be able to trust since you have already developed a business relationship.

The expertise of most insurance agents lies in their ability to present, detail and make available to you the finest policy coverage to meet your needs. Within the insurance industry, the speciality of marketing and selling does not necessarily require the agent to know about the complexities of the claims office functions. The agent can provide you with forms to initiate your claim and can refer you to the proper claims office in which to contact.

Agents are true professionals who can handle your needs in purchasing the insurance policy which is right for you, and can be available to support your claim through their interaction with the claims office manager.

DO YOU REALLY NEED THREE BIDS?

Gathering three bids is one of the insurance industry's biggest misnomers. Your policy does not call for three bids and if anyone, including your agent, suggests that this is the standard for submission on a property loss claim, he/she is probably guided by his/her honest intentions to assist you in expediting your claim.

Unless you are acting in the capacity of general contractor, where seeking multiple bids may be required in sequencing all the subcontractor work and other professionals contributing to the rebuild or repair of your home, multiple bids are not required in submitting your claim.

You will not be compensated by the insurance company for going out and soliciting multiple bids, nor will it give you any additional leverage in negotiating your claim.

The need to solicit bids will be eliminated by using a qualified restoration contractor. Consider the savings on expenses such as: Telephone, employment time loss, travel time, mileage, paid estimates, and other miscellaneous costs.

The only out-of-pocket expense you should incur is your policy's deductible. This usually ranges from $100 to $1,000. Any additional or custom work requested, which exceeds the scope of repairs and expenses approved by the insurance company, will be the responsibility of the homeowner to pay directly to the restoration contractor.

REMEMBER . . . DOCUMENT EVERYTHING!
COLLECT AND KEEP EVERYTHING PERTAINING TO YOUR CLAIM IN YOUR FILE!

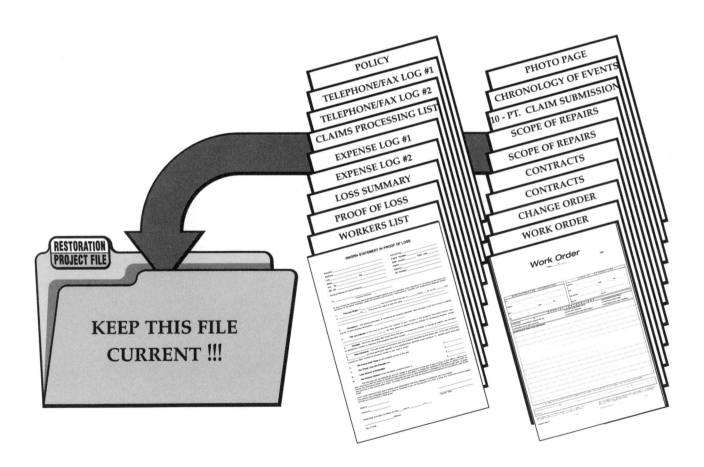

The forms above are in Chapter 16 for you to use and modify
depending on the nature of your claim.

CHAPTER 3

TEMPORARY EXPENSES

- **EMERGENCY EXPENSES - WHO PAYS?**

- **LIVING EXPENSES**

- **KEEP THOSE RECEIPTS!**

- **EARTHQUAKE!**

- **FLOOD INSURANCE**

- **EMERGENCY SERVICES**

EMERGENCY EXPENSES - WHO PAYS?

When the need for emergency services arises (normally in every emergency and insurance loss), the policyholder has two distinct options.

The first option is the homeowner can pay for emergency repairs and other immediate expenditures directly out of his/her pocket. If you are in a comfortable financial situation, this may not impact your cash flow too much. The second option is to let a qualified restoration contractor work with you in order to make necessary arrangements and to help cover the expenses for you until your claim is settled.

If you are not in the position to be advancing payment for services and expenses, the need to retain a restoration contractor is even more important.

You may be asking the question, "What's the difference between calling a handyman out to repair my roof and clean my carpet? Why would I need a restoration contractor?"

First off, companies that perform emergency services (i.e., water shutoff, boarding up of windows, temporary roof sheeting, etc.) will probably do a good job of temporary repairs, but generally are not set up to finalize permanent repairs.

Likewise, most emergency service companies do not deal regularly with insurance claims, so they demand payment immediately upon the rendering of their services.

If you need your roof, walls, carpeting, windows and/or flooring replaced or secured, you, the homeowner, will be paying these charges directly out of your pocket, and waiting for the insurance company to reimburse you.

The qualified restoration contractor can handle the paperwork and processing of emergency expenses under your policy for emergency services, and will be reimbursed by your insurance company, as a partial payment of your claim or advancement of claims pay.

A top quality restoration contractor can perform emergency services and should not demand payment until the insurance company pays for those services. This is because the restoration contractor works primarily with insurance policy claims.

Most insurance companies would prefer the same contractor providing emergency service and permanent restoration of the loss. This simplifies the claims handling and allows the insurance company to minimize its paper-shuffling and file maintenance.

LIVING EXPENSES

EVALUATING YOUR POLICY FOR LIVING EXPENSE COVERAGE

Introduction to "Loss of Use" Coverage

In addition to covering physical damage to your home, other structures, and personal property, your homeowners policy provides coverage for the loss of use of the dwelling; that is, if your home cannot be lived in as a result of a loss that is covered by your policy, most policies will pay for the increased living expenses you will incur to maintain your normal lifestyle. You are eligible for this coverage if you suffer covered damages to the extent that you must find substitute living quarters until the repairs to your home can be completed.

Obviously if your house has been totally destroyed "Loss of Use" coverage applies. If, on the other hand, your home was only partially damaged, a determination must be made as to whether this partial damage has caused your house to be unfit to live in. Certainly the loss of vital utilities such as water or electricity would render the home unlivable, just as if your kitchen or only bathroom were destroyed. Minor damage or damage to your attached garage, however, may not qualify you for this coverage. Your first step, therefore, is to come to an agreement with your claim adjuster as to whether this coverage will apply to your specific loss. Once this is determined, you must then decide which settlement option is most advantageous to you.

If it is determined that your house is uninhabitable, loss of use of your home can be calculated using two methods. The first, and most often utilized, method is called the "additional living expense" approach. The other is the "fair rental value" method. Although each insurance pol-

icy contains its own specific coverage language, we will attempt to provide you with a general description of these two settlement options. Please consult your policy to determine your insurance company's specific requirements and method of calculation.

NOTE: If you have a fire policy covering a dwelling you own and do not live in but instead rent out to others, your policy's loss of use provision probably involves settlement under the fair rental value method.

Additional Living Expense Method

If your primary residence has been completely or partially damaged by a covered peril making it unfit to live in, this coverage will reimburse you for the necessary increase in living expenses actually incurred by you so that your household can maintain its normal standard of living. The intent of this coverage is to compensate you for the difference between what your household costs would have been had there been no loss and what your costs are because of the loss.

a. Explanation of Benefit

Although specific language may vary from policy to policy, the following conditions generally apply to most homeowner policies in order for the increased expenses to be eligible for payment:

1)   they must be necessary;

2)   they must result from a covered peril, such as fire;

3)   they must be incurred by the named insured; and

4)   they must be incurred for the purpose of continuing as nearly as practical your normal standard of living prior to the loss.

In order for your claims adjuster to properly calculate your additional living expenses, it must first be determined what your household costs were prior to the loss. Those costs include utility costs, mortgage payments, food costs, real estate taxes, laundry and cleaning costs, transportation costs, and garbage disposal service costs. If the receipts for these costs were destroyed, you should make arrangements to have duplicate copies made by your mortgage company, utility company, etc. Also, credit card receipts, canceled checks, and bank statements may provide the proper substantiation of the prior costs. Once these prior costs are determined, they must be compared with the household expenses incurred during the repair period to assess whether you experienced an increase in your household expenses.

b.   Typical items covered by Additional Living Expense Coverage

1)   Extra food costs;

2)   Increased household costs;

3)   Costs of telephone or utility installation in a temporary residence;

4)   Extra transportation costs due to extra mileage to and from school or work;

5)   Relocation and storage expenses;

6)   Furniture rental for a temporary residence.

Please note that your claim for these additional expenses must be supported with receipts that show that you actually incurred the claimed expenses. Therefore, it is important to retain all receipts that document your expenditures during the repair time. Those receipts will be evaluated against your prior bills in order to determine which expenses have actually increased.

Because the Additional Living Expenses settlement option requires that all increases be supported by receipts, some situations may not be covered by this approach. As an example, if you stay with relatives during the repair period and are not charged for rent, utilities, or food, or cannot prove that you actually incurred these expenses with a receipt, you may be unable to collect insurance proceeds under this coverage option. If your situation is similar to this scenario, or you don't feel you will be able to substantiate all your expenses with receipts, you may decide to have your loss of use claim calculated on a fair rental value basis.

Fair Rental Value (FRV) Method

Rather than having to identify and substantiate which of your expenses went up or down due to your loss, you may request that the adjuster determine the fair rental value of the residence which was damaged. This will require a comparison between your residence as it existed prior to the loss and similar properties held for rental. A good source for determining the fair rental value of comparable properties is a local real estate broker who normally handles residential real estate. If the comparable value being used is for an unfurnished property, the fair rental value of furniture should be added to the calculation.

After determining the fair rental value of your home, you then subtract any expenses that do not continue dur-ing the repair period, such as landscaping services, if this cost is actually discontinued. This figure would be the amount owed to you as fair rental value.

Even under the fair rental value method, you are additionally entitled to such things as extra transportation costs, costs of telephone or utility installation in a temporary residence, and relocation expenses. Moreover, if the insurer calculates the fair rental value of your damaged home on an "unfurnished" basis, you are entitled to the cost of renting furniture for a reasonable period of time until you purchase replacement furniture.

Requirements Common to Loss of Use Claims

Certain provisions apply to all types of loss of use claims under your property policy.

a.   Time Period

Whether using the additional living expense or fair rental value method, there is a time limit on how long this coverage will last. You cannot collect on the loss of use coverage indefinitely. Payment will generally be for the shortest time required to repair or replace the damage or, if you permanently relocate, the shortest time for your household to settle elsewhere.

Therefore, you should do everything possible to ensure that reconstruction proceeds in a timely manner. Also, some policies may further restrict this coverage to a 12-month period. You should consult your policy for the exact time period conditions which apply to your claim.

b.   Policy Limit

Loss of use coverage under your homeowners policy will be limited also to either a specific dollar amount, as stated on your policy declarations, or to a certain percentage of your dwelling policy limit.

c.   Civil Authority

If a civil authority prohibits you from use of your residence premises as a result of direct damage to neighboring premises by an insured peril, the loss of use coverage will be limited to the time period the civil authority prohibits you from use of your residence premises.

Additional Loss of Use Coverage - Loss of Rent

Your policy may contain a provision covering the fair rental value of a portion of the insured property which is held for rental, such as a small cottage on the property or the unit of a duplex which you do not occupy. If you have this coverage, the fair rental value is determined by fair rental value of that portion of the property, usually the current rent, less any expenses which do not continue while the premises are not fit to inhabit.

KEEP THOSE RECEIPTS!

Again, it is stressed that you retain all bills and invoices incurred as temporary expenses as a result of your loss. When you submit your claim, those receipts will likely be evaluated against your prior bills in order to determine which expenses have actually increased.

You should also evaluate and compare your extra living expense totals, just as the insurance company will be doing.

It is a good idea to have prior bills available. For instance, if you are staying in a motel while your home is being repaired, retain a copy of your last mortgage payment to compare it to the expense to live away from your home temporarily. Find your previous month's telephone bill to compare it to the costs to make calls from the motel. Also, expect that your food costs will probably exceed your normal budget since most meals away from home will be in restaurants. Be reasonable.

EARTHQUAKE!

If you are covered for the peril of earthquake in California, the law requires that your insurer also offer you a minimum of $1,500 in loss of use benefits, specifically for additional living expenses, in the event your home becomes uninhabitable because of earthquake. Since there is an ongoing challenge by the major insurance carriers in regard to requirements for earthquake insurance, you would be wise, if you live in areas subject to this kind of loss, to check with your agent for the minimum amounts your company will pay.

In 1996, legislative developments in the State of California have created the California Earthquake Authority (CEA). This plan, underwritten by California taxpayers, has established a $10.6 billion state managed earthquake insurance program. This program is akin to the federal government sponsored flood insurance coverage program offered in flood potential communities.

Earthquake insurance coverage has always created a number of proponents, detractors and problems, and this new program is no exception. Premium rates will vary throughout the state based on high risk of earthquake prone areas (i.e., San Fernando Valley, San Francisco, etc.). The major insurance companies have also negotiated an exit clause in the agreement which allows them to drop coverage altogether should the program prove unsuccessful.

However, the insurance company's participation in the California plan must support the program for a minimum of 12 years to allow the CEA to collect enough premiums to survive a major earthquake. Be aware that, just as in any new law, this one has been untested in court and could be subject to change or modification.

FLOOD INSURANCE

Under homeowner policies, flood, overflow of streams and other bodies of water, tidal waters, waves, spray and a wide variety of other water-associated damages are excluded from any coverage whatsoever. Until 1968, virtually no flood insurance of any kind was generally available. Finally, the federal government, through the National Flood Insurance Program, stepped in with a subsidized program which offers limited amounts of flood insurance in certain areas through selected insurance companies.

The National Flood Insurance Program, administered by the Federal Emergency Management Agency (FEMA), currently offers flood insurance through the federal government and 85 private insurers. To qualify, homeowners must live in one of 18,300 flood-prone communities that have taken specific steps to control floods. Rates vary according to the structure of the house and its vulnerability to flooding.

Please take note: Homeowners that wait for a "flood alert" before getting insurance from the National Flood Insurance Program administered by FEMA will encounter a five-day waiting period between the time of purchase of the policy to the time the coverage becomes effective.

EMERGENCY SERVICES

Federal Emergency Management Agency (FEMA)

Commonly known as FEMA, the Federal Emergency Management Agency's main mission is to provide emergency relief in time of disaster. FEMA also provides consultation services, financial support and direction to assist victims of disaster with restoration and low interest loans through government programs. FEMA assistance can range from temporary housing to psychological services.

Since FEMA services are established with federal guidelines of mobility and service, assistance by this department is not readily available without their involvement in a major disaster. However, information is available outlining the services provided and supplemental programs by contacting the **Federal Emergency Management Agency (FEMA) in Washington, D.C. at 202-646-2400.**

Small Business Administration (SBA)

Originally established to provide entrepreneurial support, the SBA has been incorporated into the federal government assistance programs regarding disasters. If you are a victim of a major disaster (i.e., fire, hurricane, tornado, etc.) you may, through the FEMA programs of assistance, apply for a low interest loan to rebuild your property through the SBA. The SBA maintains a fund for the express purpose of providing assistance to victims of disasters. Information concerning disaster relief is available by contacting the **Small Business Administration at 202-606-4000.**

American Red Cross Emergency Services

American Red Cross Emergency Services offer relief following a natural disaster, such as a hurricane, earthquake or flood.

The American Red Cross Emergency Services assist victims of natural disasters with food, clothing and shelter. They also establish information centers to help victims contact medical and psychological services and determine whether or not these services are available through federally funded programs. The American Red Cross Emergency Services may be contacted through the **American Red Cross headquarters at 703-206-6000.**

State Emergency Services

Your own state also provides emergency relief services. State emergency services are often directly tied to the state's Armed Forces Reserve Centers. Telephone numbers may usually be found in your local telephone directory under "State of (your state) Emergency Services."

CHAPTER 4
ASSESSING YOUR POLICY AND DAMAGE

- **WHAT CAUSED YOUR LOSS? - WHAT WAS THE RESULTANT DAMAGE?**

- **WHAT IS A PERIL?**

- **WHAT'S AN "ALL RISK" POLICY?**

- **TYPES OF LOSSES**

- **PROXIMATE CAUSE DOCTRINE**

- **DECLARATIONS PAGE**

- **TYPES OF HOMEOWNERS POLICIES**

- **WHAT HOMEOWNER POLICIES COVER**

- **COVERED ROOF PERILS**

- **REPAIRABLE DAMAGE**

- **SOME TYPICAL EXCLUSIONS**

- **ASBESTOS ABATEMENT**

- **LEAD-BASED PAINT LAW**

- **SAMPLE OF A REPLACEMENT COST POLICY**

Property insurance is usually divided into two types, real and personal. Real property refers to land and the things attached permanently to it, like a house or garage. Personal property refers to things not attached to the land such as appliances, clothes, furniture and so forth.

A homeowner's policy protects your house or dwelling. Other structures on your property, such as a tool shed, guest house, or detached garage, should also be covered. These are called appurtenant structures. Appurtenant structures are usually insured for up to 10 percent of the coverage on the house. There is generally no coverage for buildings on your property used for commercial purposes or for buildings that you rent to others, except for garages. Personal property is also generally covered under your homeowners policy. It usually includes household items and other belongings owned by you and your family, whether lost at home or away from home. You can also buy protection that covers the personal property of your guests, while they are visiting.

When reviewing your policy, note if a term or condition of your insurance policy is ambiguous or indefinite. The courts have often upheld that the issue of doubt should go in favor of the insured since the insurance company was the sole creator of the policy language. Also, note that your policy likely states . . .
"When a policy provision is in conflict with the applicable law of the State in which this policy is issued, the law of the State will apply."

WHAT CAUSED YOUR LOSS? WHAT WAS THE RESULTANT DAMAGE?

Some policyholders assess the resultant damage to determine the cause of their loss, but resultant damage is not always easily traceable to the initial source of the damage.

Some causes of the resultant damage are obvious. The source of the damage can be tracked to the results without intrusion (i.e., breaking into a wall to discover damage, jackhammering concrete foundations to discover leakage, etc.). Sometimes the obvious source of the damage is not covered under your policy, but the resultant damage is covered.

For example, a broken pipe may be the cause of your loss, but the resultant damage is water-soaked carpet, or water-damaged walls or ceilings. In this case, the broken pipe may not be a covered loss (depending on the cause of the break), and you would need to absorb the cost of repair to the pipe. However, the resultant damage (i.e., to carpets, walls, ceilings, etc.) should be covered, along with the intrusive work required (breaking into walls, floors, etc.) to get to the damaged area and service the needed repairs.

Some sources of damage are more difficult to ascertain and determine than others. Let's say a storm blew a door open in your home allowing rain to enter the premises. The next morning the storm was gone, but the resultant damage was water-soaked carpeting adjacent to the open door. In this case the source of the damage, the storm, had moved on and the difficulty of determining that it was the source of your damage was only evident by the water-soaked carpeting which remained.

Another example is wind-blown damage. If, for instance, a severe rain/wind storm blows shingles off of the roof of your home, causing rain to damage the interior or the contents inside, both the roof and the interior damage would be covered. Since damage by wind-driven rain is a covered peril in your policy (unless it is specifically excluded), the cause <u>and</u> the resultant damage would be covered in most cases.

PROXIMATE CAUSE DOCTRINE

The Proximate Cause Doctrine means that if initial damage causes further damage by an unbroken chain of events, and the initial cause is covered under your policy, the resultant damage should also be covered.

For example, if you have suffered intrusion to your roof due to wind and severe rain, the wind/rain initially caused the damage to your roof (proximate cause). You may have also sustained damage to your walls and ceilings as a result of the intrusion to your roof, which allowed water to seep into your walls and ceilings (resultant damage). The roof damage is usually covered by your insurance policy under the "perils" provision. The wall and ceiling damage fall under the common law civil interpretation of proximate cause. Since the cause of the initial damage should be covered under "covered perils," and the resultant loss suffered is a result of that damage, the resultant damage shall also be covered within the policy provisions.

Courts have traditionally ruled that if the proximate cause of a loss is a covered peril, then the entire loss is covered even though excluded perils may come into play during the sequence of events. For example, if wind uproots a tree, and the earth movement raises the foundation of your garage, then the coverage for earth movement is an exclusion, but the coverage for wind damage is not. The wind damage was the initial force, put into action, that caused the loss, and the resultant foundational damage should be covered.

WHAT IS A PERIL?

A peril is a natural event (wind, rain, snow, etc.) which may cause damage covered by an insurance carrier, provided you have purchased the necessary protection through valid coverage.

WHAT'S AN "ALL RISK" POLICY?

All risk coverage means that it protects against loss by any cause, except those items specifically excluded.

TYPES OF LOSSES

Fire

Fire losses can create an abundance of problems. Your home may be uninhabitable, and the security of your personal belongings may be in jeopardy.

If the fire department uses water to extinguish the fire, damage by the water may be prevalent throughout the dwelling. You and your family may not be able to return to your home.

You should seek the service of a qualified emergency restoration company at once.

As previously mentioned, these companies can board up windows, secure the premises and shut off water and power to avoid further damage to your home. Fire losses can cause secondary damage such as smoke damage, water damage, and structural and foundational weakness.

Wind/Rain Damage

Perhaps the most common type of loss is wind damage and associated rain damage. Wind and rain can cause an enormous amount of damage to, in particular, the roof of your home. Wood shingles, clay tiles, and composite roof coverings are all susceptible to damage and can cause other wind/rain-related damage to ceilings, walls, floors, furniture, and appliances. Wet spots or discoloration of walls and/or ceilings are often a telltale sign that there may be a roof leak.

Falling Objects

Damage caused by falling objects could include anything from a falling tree branch to an aircraft engine or even the aircraft itself. In fact, there is not much that would fall out of the sky and cause damage to a roof that isn't covered under property insurance policies. Any interior structural damage that occurs as a result of something falling out of the sky is usually covered also.

Broken Pipes

Water pipes can break at anytime. New homes or older homes can experience this kind of problem. Piping that is most vulnerable to breakage are overhead pipes that may fracture with foundational shifts, or during an earthquake or aftershocks. Older pipe placement and fixtures, primarily those made of galvanized metal, can deteriorate and break within walls and flooring. Again, wet spots or discoloration of walls and/or ceilings can be a sign that a water pipe has cracked or fractured. Breakage can also occur during freezing of plumbing components.

Weight of Snow and Ice

Obviously, losses caused by snow and/or ice concern roofs and structural components of your home. Snow and ice can produce tremendous pressure and weight on the roof of your home and can cause breakage and fracture primary beams, walls, window frames and dislodge door jambs.

Smoke Damage

Smoke damage can emanate from a variety of sources. Fireplaces with closed flues can cause extensive damage. Electrical fires can cause major smoke damage and are very dangerous to control. Ceilings, walls, floors and doors can usually be restored and cleaned by a competent restoration contractor.

Vandalism or Malicious Mischief

A loss that occurs by vandalism or malicious mischief can be very traumatic to the homeowner and their family. This kind of loss is also criminal conduct and should be reported to the police, as well as to the insurance company or agent at the earliest time possible.

Breakage of Glass

Breakage of glass is the proverbial "baseball through the window" type of claim. Normally, a loss that involves breakage of glass (unless major in severity) is a claim that is recognized, evaluated, and paid by the insurance company with little resistance because of the small monetary exposure.

Theft

Akin to the emotional trauma of vandalism and malicious mischief, theft must be reported immediately to the police. If you are prepared with an inventory of the missing items and pictures and/or video taken before the theft, you'll be way ahead of the game.

Collapse of Building

The collapse of a building is usually associated with earthquake damage. A structural collapse can, however, happen at any time. This type of loss is sometimes contested by insurance companies, and delayed by a long investigation and evaluation.

Hot Water Heater

The rupture of a hot water heater is a dangerous situation and a very common loss. It can result in serious injury and property damage. Never attempt to curtail the flow of scalding water if the path of the water flow is in the area of the shutoff valve. If this is the case, turn off the water to the entire house at the main water valve outside.

PERSONAL LIABILITY CLAIMS

Standard homeowner policies generally include coverage for comprehensive personal liability. Under Section II of the policy, a standard amount of $25,000 in coverage is provided for general liability.

For instance, if your neighbor's giant backyard oak tree grows to monumental heights, and the roots creep over your property line and raise your fence and crack your driveway then, assuming that your neighbor is insured, you can file a claim against his personal liability coverage.

Similarly, your neighbor can also file a claim against you for a like incident.

Personal liability coverage is intended to protect policyholders from paying for mishaps for which they are liable. They generally cover the amount that policyholders become legally liable to pay because of bodily injury or property damage.

If you are unable to file a claim against your neighbor's insurance policy, you may elect to file a claim with your own insurance carrier.

If your insurance company pays your claim immediately, before you have filed directly against your neighbor's insurance company, you may be asked to sign a document known as an "Assignment of Subrogation Rights."

Subrogation allows your insurance company to pay you for your claim against the other party immediately. The subrogation rights then allow your insurance company to pursue the negligent party or their insurance company directly to recover the money that was paid to you.

Under personal liability:

• The insurance company is often obligated to defend and indemnify the policyholder against claims and suits, within the policy's coverage, whether or not the allegations are true.

• The insurance company, under terms of the standard policy, often has the right to settle a claim without the consent of the policyholder.

DECLARATIONS PAGE

Separate from the body of the policy ("Terms and Conditions"), and usually attached to the front of your policy, is the Declarations Page (commonly known as the "dec sheet" or "dec page"). The Declarations Page lists the name(s) of the insured, effective dates of the policy, expiration date, dollar amounts of coverage, supplemental coverage and the deductible amount.

The Declarations Page also names your mortgage holder or lender. When your insurance company finalizes the settlement draft concerning your loss, they will usually include your mortgage holder as a payee, because of the mutual interest in the property.

DECLARATIONS PAGE LEGEND
(example on next page)

1. Your policy number.
2. This is the insurable interest party.
3. This is the effective period of your insurance coverage. Your policy's expiration date is also noted.
4. Amount of total coverage available for the complete restoration of your home.
5. This covers structures detached from the primary dwelling (i.e., detached garage, guest house, tool shed, etc.).
6. This covers your personal property contained inside your home. It should also cover personal property damaged or stolen while you are away from your home.
7. This covers loss of use. When your home becomes uninhabitable due to extensive damage (i.e., from fire, etc.), this part of the policy would cover you for living expenses and expenses to cover immediate emergency repairs to your property.
8. This covers you for any damages you are obligated to pay, caused by you, and results in bodily injury or property damage to another party.
9. This covers medical payments for any person injured on your property.
10. These are additions to your policy coverage known as "endorsements." These are separate insurance policies to cover specific items.
11. This is your lender's name. All claim settlement checks will have this company named as a payee.
12. This is the amount which must be exceeded in damage cost before your insurance company becomes liable.
13. Discounts that are applicable (i.e., home burglar alarms, nonsmoker, mature policyholder, long-time insured, etc.).
14. Your agent's name and telephone number.

THE DECLARATIONS PAGE

(usually found attached to the front of your policy)

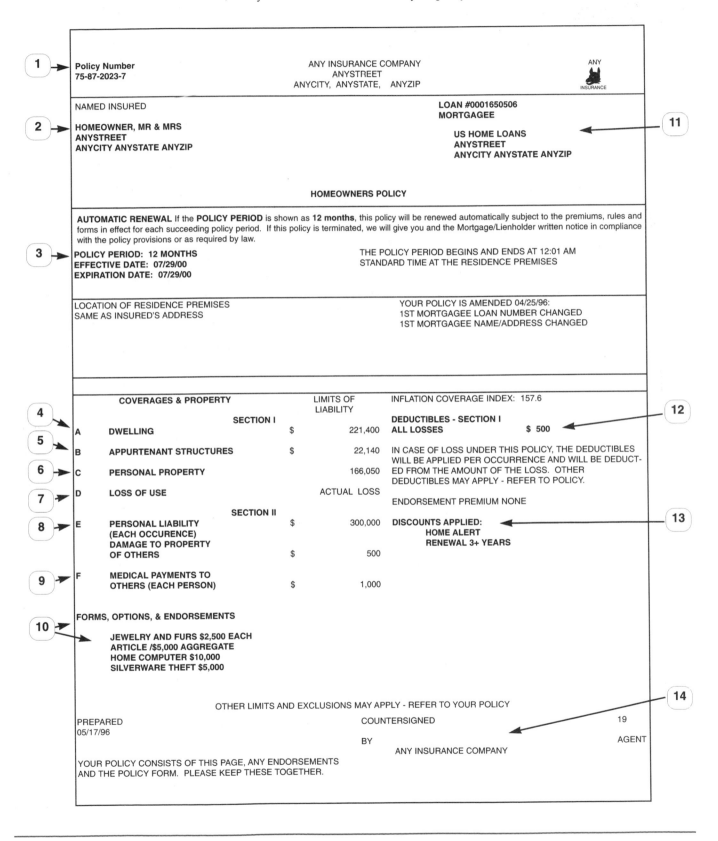

1 → Policy Number
75-87-2023-7

ANY INSURANCE COMPANY
ANYSTREET
ANYCITY, ANYSTATE,   ANYZIP

ANY
INSURANCE

NAMED INSURED

2 → HOMEOWNER, MR & MRS
ANYSTREET
ANYCITY ANYSTATE ANYZIP

LOAN #0001650506
MORTGAGEE

US HOME LOANS
ANYSTREET
ANYCITY ANYSTATE ANYZIP

← **11**

HOMEOWNERS POLICY

AUTOMATIC RENEWAL If the **POLICY PERIOD** is shown as **12 months**, this policy will be renewed automatically subject to the premiums, rules and forms in effect for each succeeding policy period. If this policy is terminated, we will give you and the Mortgage/Lienholder written notice in compliance with the policy provisions or as required by law.

3 → **POLICY PERIOD: 12 MONTHS**
EFFECTIVE DATE: 07/29/00
EXPIRATION DATE: 07/29/00

THE POLICY PERIOD BEGINS AND ENDS AT 12:01 AM
STANDARD TIME AT THE RESIDENCE PREMISES

LOCATION OF RESIDENCE PREMISES
SAME AS INSURED'S ADDRESS

YOUR POLICY IS AMENDED 04/25/96:
1ST MORTGAGEE LOAN NUMBER CHANGED
1ST MORTGAGEE NAME/ADDRESS CHANGED

	COVERAGES & PROPERTY	LIMITS OF LIABILITY	

INFLATION COVERAGE INDEX: 157.6

4 →
5 →
6 →
7 →
8 →
9 →

SECTION I

A	DWELLING	$ 221,400	
B	APPURTENANT STRUCTURES	$ 22,140	
C	PERSONAL PROPERTY	166,050	
D	LOSS OF USE	ACTUAL LOSS	

SECTION II

E	PERSONAL LIABILITY (EACH OCCURENCE)	$ 300,000	
	DAMAGE TO PROPERTY OF OTHERS	$ 500	
F	MEDICAL PAYMENTS TO OTHERS (EACH PERSON)	$ 1,000	

DEDUCTIBLES - SECTION I
ALL LOSSES   **$ 500**   ← **12**

IN CASE OF LOSS UNDER THIS POLICY, THE DEDUCTIBLES WILL BE APPLIED PER OCCURRENCE AND WILL BE DEDUCTED FROM THE AMOUNT OF THE LOSS. OTHER DEDUCTIBLES MAY APPLY - REFER TO POLICY.

ENDORSEMENT PREMIUM NONE

DISCOUNTS APPLIED: ← **13**
    HOME ALERT
    RENEWAL 3+ YEARS

FORMS, OPTIONS, & ENDORSEMENTS

10 →
JEWELRY AND FURS $2,500 EACH
ARTICLE /$5,000 AGGREGATE
HOME COMPUTER $10,000
SILVERWARE THEFT $5,000

OTHER LIMITS AND EXCLUSIONS MAY APPLY - REFER TO YOUR POLICY

PREPARED
05/17/96

COUNTERSIGNED   19

BY   AGENT
        ANY INSURANCE COMPANY

← **14**

YOUR POLICY CONSISTS OF THIS PAGE, ANY ENDORSEMENTS AND THE POLICY FORM. PLEASE KEEP THESE TOGETHER.

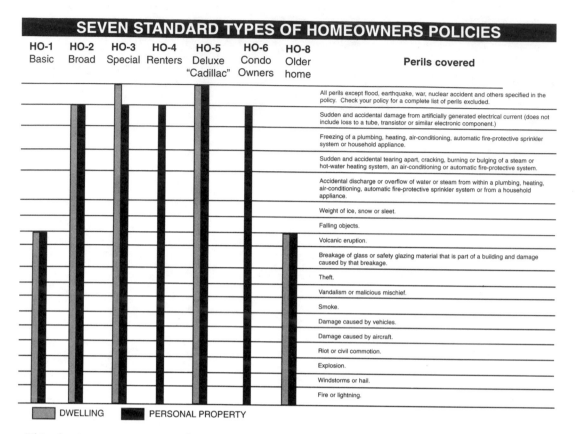

SEVEN STANDARD TYPES OF HOMEOWNERS POLICIES

HO-1 Basic	HO-2 Broad	HO-3 Special	HO-4 Renters	HO-5 Deluxe "Cadillac"	HO-6 Condo Owners	HO-8 Older home	Perils covered
							All perils except flood, earthquake, war, nuclear accident and others specified in the policy. Check your policy for a complete list of perils excluded.
							Sudden and accidental damage from artificially generated electrical current (does not include loss to a tube, transistor or similar electronic component.)
							Freezing of a plumbing, heating, air-conditioning, automatic fire-protective sprinkler system or household appliance.
							Sudden and accidental tearing apart, cracking, burning or bulging of a steam or hot-water heating system, an air-conditioning or automatic fire-protective system.
							Accidental discharge or overflow of water or steam from within a plumbing, heating, air-conditioning, automatic fire-protective sprinkler system or from a household appliance.
							Weight of ice, snow or sleet.
							Falling objects.
							Volcanic eruption.
							Breakage of glass or safety glazing material that is part of a building and damage caused by that breakage.
							Theft.
							Vandalism or malicious mischief.
							Smoke.
							Damage caused by vehicles.
							Damage caused by aircraft.
							Riot or civil commotion.
							Explosion.
							Windstorms or hail.
							Fire or lightning.

DWELLING   PERSONAL PROPERTY

This chart represents a general compilation of the standard multi-state insurance policy offerings. It does not include specific exclusions that are subject to individual policies and certain areas of the U.S.A.

TYPES OF HOMEOWNERS POLICIES

In the 1950's, the insurance industry introduced a series of packaged policies which were developed to provide homeowners with broader and more economical coverage than had previously been available.

Homeowners policies have grown in popularity and have all but replaced individual policies for owners of one and two family homes. At the present time, home-owner policies can be obtained in every state but Mississippi, where a similar package is offered under the name "Comprehensive Dwelling Policy."

Insurance companies currently offer six different homeowners policies, with certain variations of coverage and exclusions designated HO-1, 2, 3, 4, 5 and 6. According to the Insurance Information Institute, the HO-1 and HO-2 used to be the most frequently written of all homeowners policies. An HO-1, the Basic Form, covers eleven perils. The HO-2, the Broad Form, covers seventeen different perils. The most common of all

homeowners policies is the HO-3. It is a policy which provides an all risk and replacement cost coverage to your home. Personal property is insured against named perils, as indicated in the policy. These perils are the same as the ones listed in the HO-2 policy, although moderately modified.

What sets the HO-3 apart from the HO-1 and HO-2 is that it offers all risk coverage on the dwelling. This all risk policy would cover, among other things, the leaking of rainwater into the interior of a dwelling through a worn roof even though there had been no damage to the roof by wind. Accidental spillage of paint on carpeting would be covered, as well as accidental burns on a kitchen counter-top where no fire is involved. The HO-3 policy typically costs 10 to 15 percent more than the HO-1 policy.

HO-4 covers personal property and is intended for those who rent an apartment or home. It also affords personal liability coverage and medical payments to others. HO-6 is intended for condominium owners.

HO-1, 2, 3, and 5 are for owners of one and two family homes and have a format, as follows:

Section I Coverage

A. applies to the dwelling

B. applies to appurtenant structures on the premises other than the dwelling

C. applies to unscheduled personal property

D. applies to additional living expenses

Section II Coverage

E. applies to personal liability

F. applies to medical payments to others

Section I differs among the individual policies in the perils that are insured. Section II is identical under most forms in the liability insurance offered.

SECTION I

A. The dwelling. This is the structure described in the policy. It could be a house, a bungalow and so on. It includes an attached garage, if there is one, and any other structures attached to the dwelling. Heating, plumbing and electrical fixtures that are part of the dwelling are also included in Coverage A. The dwelling must be used primarily as a private residence.

B. Appurtenant structures are other structures on the premises not in contact with the dwelling. These may include a storage shed, detached garage, workshop, and so on, provided these are not used for business purposes.

C. Unscheduled personal property is usually described as the "contents." It is called "unscheduled" because the contents are grouped within a broad general category without listing specific items. It includes furniture, clothing, books, appliances, and other personal property.

D. Additional living expenses. If the dwelling becomes uninhabitable because of a loss covered in the policy, the insurance company will pay the costs of living above what the insured normally spends. In addition, coverage D includes the loss of rental value for a garage, the second apartment of a two family dwelling or a portion of the dwelling used or held for rental.

SECTION II

Standard homeowners policies afford the same coverage in Section II, however, increases in coverage can be added.

E. Personal liability. You are insured for up to $25,000 if you or a member of your family accidentally injures someone or damages someone's property and he or she, in turn, sues you. You are protected both on and off the premises for a wide variety of mishaps. For example, you are protected if someone injures his or herself by falling down your front stairs, or by slipping on your sidewalk, or even if your dog runs down the street and bites the mailman. Be aware that coverage and civil liability varies from state to state.

F. Medical payments. If a person is injured on your property, generally medical expenses up to $500 are covered. In addition, some off-the-premises injuries are also covered. For example, if your golf ball strikes and injures another golfer, the insurer will pay for the injury.

WHAT HOMEOWNER POLICIES COVER

The HO-1 policy, as written by the Insurance Services Office, is generally the least expensive policy for homeowners. Known as the "basic form," it insures the dwelling, appurtenant structures, and contents against eleven different perils:

1. Fire or lightning.

2. Windstorms or hail.

3. Explosion.

4. Riot or civil commotion.

5. Damage caused by aircraft.

6. Damage caused by vehicles.

7. Smoke.

8. Vandalism or malicious mischief.

9. Theft.

10. Breakage of glass or safety glazing material that is part of a building and damage caused by that breakage.

11. Volcanic eruption.

The HO-2 policy expands the coverage of the HO-1 to include the following additional perils:

12. Falling objects.

13. Weight of ice, snow or sleet.

14. Accidental discharge or overflow of water or steam from within a plumbing, heating, air-conditioning,

automatic fire-protective sprinkler system or from a household appliance.

15. Sudden and accidental tearing apart, cracking, burning, or bulging of a steam or hot-water heating system, an air-conditioning or automatic fire-protective system.

16. Freezing of a plumbing, heating, air-conditioning, automatic fire-protective sprinkler system or household appliance.

17. Sudden and accidental damage from artificially generated electrical current (does not include loss to a tube, transistor or similar electronic component).

The HO-3 policy increases coverage on the dwelling and appurtenant structures to an "all risk" basis and insures the contents for the named perils on the HO-2. The term "all risk" is a misnomer, because there is a list of exceptions and conditions on the policy which makes it anything but "all risk." This policy limits coverage of personal property to the 17 perils included in the broad form (HO-2).

The HO-4 policy applies only to personal property and is specifically intended for apartment dwellers or persons renting a house. It insures the contents against virtually all the perils insured against in the HO-2 policy.

The HO-5 policy is the so-called "Cadillac" of homeowners policies. It insures the dwelling, appurtenant structures, and contents against all perils except those specifically excluded: Flood, earthquake, war and nuclear attack.

After the California earthquake of 1994, the Department of Insurance ordered the major insurance companies to offer earthquake insurance in the southern California area. Most, if not all, of the major insurance companies declined to follow this order and many have decided to eliminate homeowners insurance completely in some of the liability exposed areas.

The HO-6 policy is the most recent of the homeowners policies. It specifically covers the personal property of condominium unit owners and includes an additional living expense allowance. The perils insured against

are similar to those in the HO-2 policy. This is a separate policy which covers your personal property, not structural damage, and covered under a different policy which may be required by your C,C&Rs (Covenants, Conditions, & Restrictions).

The obsolete HO-8 (Older Home Insurance) policy provided for damage to a building to be paid for on the basis of Actual Cash Value (ACV) without deduction for depreciation if the policyholder carried insurance for at least 80 percent of the replacement costs.

Older homes, however, usually are so constructed that it is not economically feasible to duplicate them following a loss. The HO-8 policy was designed to aid these homeowners by allowing them to carry lower limits of insurance, such as the market value of the home, rather than the 80 percent of replacement cost used for newer houses. In effect, the policy contemplated returning the property to serviceable condition, but not necessarily with the use of materials of the same kind and quality as the original.

It has been asked why there is a number designated at the end of the homeowner policy type. It merely designates the edition of the policy. In the past, there used to be HO-1s and HO-2s, but agents these days sell almost exclusively the standard homeowner policy known as the HO-3 policy. The lower numbered policies provide less coverage than the higher numbered policies.

The HO-3 policy is, by far, the most popular coverage among homeowners, and is the leading seller within the insurance industry.

Actual Cash Value (ACV)

Actual cash value is generally defined as fair market value.

The fair market value of an item is the amount at which a knowledgeable buyer (under no unusual pressure) would be willing to buy, and a knowledgeable seller (under no unusual pressure) would be willing to sell. However, if there is really no functioning market for an item, then replacement cost minus depreciation should be used to determine value.

TIP: When reviewing your policy to see what it says, it is just as important to see what it doesn't say. For example: A homeowner recently had a claim for roof damage that was caused by a raccoon. The homeowners policy stated that if damage was caused by birds, vermin, rodents, insects or domestic animals then the damages would not be covered. However, a raccoon is considered a mammal and, because the policy did not specifically exclude mammals, it was a covered loss and the homeowner was given an entire new roof.

If you suffered a total loss to your home, the actual cash value should be determined by the fair market value of your home at the time of your loss, less the value of the land.

If you suffered a partial loss to your home and repairs are necessary, the loss should be paid by determining the cost to replace the damaged area minus depreciation. The same measure is used to determine actual cash value of lost or damaged contents.

Depreciation is usually determined by calculating the difference between how long the item was in use against its life expectancy. Insurance companies have guidelines which can be used for this purpose; however, it is important to understand that there is considerable variation in determining the life expectancy of an item and the guidelines should be adjusted accordingly.

An actual cash value policy will provide the fair market value of the dwelling (at total loss) or the damaged portion of the dwelling (at partial loss) up to the amount of money shown on the declarations page as the limit of liability for the structure. These limits, originally determined by the insured and the agent, are presumed to reflect the fair market value and not the replacement cost of the structure. The policy limits are arrived at by a real estate appraisal of the property as a whole minus the appraised value of the land.

Replacement Cost

Replacement cost is the cost of replacing lost or damaged property with new property of "like kind and quality" at current prices.

A replacement cost policy will provide the amount of money necessary to repair or replace the dwelling in like kind and quality, but only up to the amount of money shown on the declarations page as limits of liability for the structure. Purchase of this policy presumes that the structure is insured for less than 80% of its replacement cost. When the structure is insured for less than 80% of its replacement cost, a co-insurance penalty may apply.

Guaranteed Replacement Cost (GRC)

Guaranteed replacement cost is an insurance term and refers to coverage and dwelling policy limits. If you purchased guaranteed replacement cost coverage and all conditions required by the insurance contract are met, you would be entitled to be paid for the full replacement cost of your home if you suffered a total loss. You would be entitled to this settlement even if your dwelling policy limits were less that the cost to replace your home.

A guaranteed replacement cost policy will provide for the rebuilding or replacement of the lost dwelling, in like kind and quality, no matter what the cost, regardless of policy limits. At purchase, the structure is presumed to be insured at the outset of the policy to 100% of its replacement cost, as determined by the insurer.

Beware: Some companies will guarantee the replacement cost only if one rebuilds and does not purchase a replacement dwelling; if the choice is made to replace the destroyed structure with an already built house, or to rebuild at a site other than the site of the loss, you may only be able to recoup the actual cash value of the lost dwelling, which is generally much less that it costs to rebuild.

Beware: Some so-called "guaranteed" replacement cost policies actually guarantee costs only to a certain percentage above the limits on the declarations page. In other words, there is a "cap" on the limit of liability. These policies are now referred to, instead, as "extended replacement cost" policies.

It should be noted, too, that the value of the dwelling under any of the above policies does not include the value of the land the structure is sitting on.

Building Code Upgrade (Ordinance or Law) Coverage

The phrase above, "the lost dwelling," is underlined for an important reason. Building codes periodically change to conform to ever-rising safety and environmental standards. You can bet that the codes have changed to some extent since your house was built, unless it was brand new when the loss occurred. Unless there is additional coverage for building code upgrades in your policy, you may have to incur non-reimbursable expenses to build in compliance with present codes. Such coverage appears as an "endorsement" — that is, as an option for "ordinance or law" coverage — for a small added premium.

While electrical or plumbing code changes may not cost much, foundation costs can be very high. Firestorm damage can be unique in that temperatures may be high enough to destroy foundations and retaining walls. The "usual" solitary home fire, however, might not do so. By contrast, damage to foundations could be expected in the event of an earthquake.

The endorsement providing code upgrade coverage generally is not so expensive as to be unaffordable to the average homeowner. In California for example since July 1993, the law has required the insurer or agent to disclose its existence when selling new policies. As of January 1, 1994, the insurer has to make the disclosure at the first renewal of existing policies. Check your policy to see if you are covered.

COVERED ROOF PERILS

Wind damage and associated roof damage, according to insurance statistical sources, is the number one claim filed under property damage protection nationwide.

You will find, however, that not all roof repairs will have the financial support of your insurance company. Most homeowner insurance policies cover the same roof perils. It is important for you to know which roof perils are covered in the property insurance policy you are purchasing.

Wind Damage:

Perhaps the most common covered peril in property insurance policies is wind damage. This type of damage will usually trigger coverage; therefore, the insurance company should pay for the repairs less the insured's deductible. The insurance deductible in every type of property insurance policy is that amount of the total cost of repairs that the insured is to pay. The insurance company, therefore, pays the remaining balance after the deductible. If the total cost of repairs is $5,500.00, and the insured's deductible is $250.00, then the insurance company will pay the repair contractor and the insured $5,250.00 and the insured will pay the contractor directly his or her deductible of $250.00.

Falling Objects:

There is usually no exclusion for falling objects that cause damage to a roof. This kind of damage could occur from a falling tree branch or from an aircraft engine, for example. In fact, there is practically nothing that could fall out of the sky and cause damage to a roof that isn't covered under property insurance policies. Any interior structural damages that occur as a result usually are also covered. If, for instance, your baby grand piano is covered and is damaged as a result of rain intrusion from the hole in your roof caused by a falling tree, you most likely are covered. However, if roof repairs are in progress and parts of the roof are open and rain causes damage to your baby grand piano, you may not be covered under your homeowners policy.

Weight of Snow and Ice:

You may have to hire a contractor to repair a roof that has been damaged by the weight of snow or ice. Most homeowner insurance policies do, in fact, cover these types of damages. Internal water damage to the roof, if it leaks, may also be covered.

REPAIRABLE DAMAGE

Most property policies cover multiple damages if they occur at the same time. If high winds open up a portion or all of a structure and rain enters which causes collateral damages, then such damages are covered. That means that any part of the interior structure damaged by rain should also be covered by the owner's insurance carrier, except for the deductible, if reasonable attempts have been made to mitigate damages.

An insurance company's responsibility is to restore the building owner's loss, as covered under the policy limits. That means that the carrier should pay for whatever repairs are necessary to bring the property back to the way it was before the loss, absent any separate endorsements. At least that is the theory. You will encounter some adjusters who will disagree with you as to the extent of the actual damages. The key note in such a situation is "diplomacy." Many adjusters are quite willing to change their minds if you rationally and politely demonstrate to them the basis of your opinion. If you convince them, well and good. If not, there are other means available to you that will assist you if a genuine disagreement develops during the course of your damage assessment or during the course of repairs. This will be discussed in greater detail in Chapter 10 entitled, "THE ADJUSTER."

Mold and Mildew

Typically, mold and mildew are not covered under property insurance policies, however, there are occasions when such damage is covered. For example, if rain damage affects a dwelling, and a period of time transpires (which is not the fault of the insured) between the time of the loss and the time the insured reports it to his/her insurance company, then mildew damage that occurs as a result of the rain leaks may be covered. A typical example would be mildew that is found behind kitchen cabinets after a roof leaks, and the damage is not discovered until after the homeowner has severe allergic reactions.

Damages to Ceilings and Walls

Most of your collateral damages due to roof leaks will involve ceilings and walls. The extent of repairs, of course, will be based on the severity of damage.

Ceiling repairs will usually be limited in nature to the areas affected, especially acoustic ("cottage cheese") ceilings. Depending upon the severity of damage, your "scope of repairs" (see Chapter 8) will entail only that amount of damage that is visible.

Of course, if all or even a part of the acoustic ceiling is coming down or bowing due to excessive exposure to water, then it may be wise to propose replacing most, if not all, of that ceiling.

If the ceiling is drywall and smooth, then any repairs to the drywall will automatically entail repainting the ceiling. Since most "touch-ups" are quite visible, it might be necessary to repaint the entire ceiling to make it look as uniform in color and consistency as it did before the loss.

Follow this rule of thumb: If there are no breaks in the surface of the ceiling or wall, the paint should continue until there is a definite break. Such breaks will be obvious, such as door jambs, walls, etc. If an adjoining room ceiling is not damaged, then it will not be necessary to repaint it. This is in keeping with the "continuous" or "line of sight" theory which should be followed by all property insurance adjusters. "Line of Sight" is discussed further in Chapter 8.

Follow the same principle with respect to rain damage to walls. For repairs that involve repairing or replacing sections of drywall, considerable repainting may be necessary. It is not unusual to have to repaint entire adjoining rooms, such as living and dining rooms, kitchens and hallways, or landings that extend to and match adjoining living rooms, especially the vaulted ceiling variety.

Damages to Flooring

Of course, all types of flooring can be just as affected by rain damage. Certain types of flooring that have been damaged will require different types of repairs. If your carpet has been affected, then it would be prudent to hire a qualified restoration contractor who will conduct immediate emergency repairs to the carpet. A quick response could save your carpet.

If carpet has been allowed to sit in water or moisture too long, then it may begin to delaminate, mildew or furniture stains will develop (the most common type of carpet damage). If such is the case, then the carpet may have to be replaced.

Usually, the property adjuster will want to see the carpet before it is ripped up and disposed of in order to determine any attempts at cleaning. You may observe the damage yourself and determine a cleaning and deodorizing attempt is all that is necessary. If the cleaning does not remove the stains, then the carpet will have to be replaced. Your clean up attempt, as well as the replacement of the carpet, should still be covered by the insurance company. That is why it is important to let the insurance adjuster view the carpet beforehand, otherwise the adjuster may question the necessity of cleaning the carpet in the first place if you determine later that it must be replaced. If it is not possible to let your adjuster view the damaged carpet, be sure to take pictures before and after cleaning.

Other types of flooring, such as wood floors, require a bit more care. It would be wise to hire a wood floor expert to first examine the floor and make any recommendations before it is simply ripped up. Of course, the company adjuster will want to examine the damage due to its high cost to replace wood flooring. Sanding and refinishing one section of wood flooring requires the sanding and refinishing of all of the flooring if it is continuous and in the "line of sight." If the wood floors cannot be sanded or screened to match new wood floors, then total wood floor replacement throughout may be necessary.

Vinyl and vinyl flooring tile can buckle if water and/or moisture gets underneath it. It may also be necessary to replace or tie down the sub-flooring.

Marble floors rarely need to be replaced unless the water damage is so severe that the cleaning attempt fails. The majority of the time you will find that all that is necessary is acid washing and polishing.

Linoleum can be difficult to match, so total replacement is usually necessary. Again, the continuous and "line of site" theory is observed (see Chapter 8).

TIP: When reviewing your policy to see what it says, it is just as important to see what it doesn't say.

For example: Another homeowner recently had a claim that a wind storm had blown down a tree in the homeowners front yard and it was going to cost several hundred dollars to have it removed. Under the normal exclusions of the policy, the tree removal would not be covered but, because the tree had brushed up against the house causing minor damage to the edge of the roof, it became a covered loss.

SOME TYPICAL EXCLUSIONS

Water Damage:

This type of exclusion involves water damage that occurs from surface or sub-surface water. This is typical for all types of floods that occur from excess rains, rivers or lakes overflowing their banks, tidal waves and the like. It also includes subterranean water that bubbles up from below the ground and into the dwelling. Usually the water will enter the walls, doors or under the slab (if not on a raised foundation). This exclusion also deals with sewers that back up and cause damages inside the dwelling; however, this only applies if the sewage line that backed up originated in the main city line, usually located out in the street. If such a sewage backup occurs along the line within the property limits of the homeowner, then there is usually coverage under the owner's property insurance policy.

Earth Movement:

Generally, this type of loss is caused by, resulting from, contributed to or aggravated by earthquake, landslide, mudflow, earth sinking, rising and/or shifting or volcanic eruption (meaning the eruption, explosion or effusion of a volcano). Any loss of this nature is not usually covered with the exception of earthquake, provided that the homeowner has purchased a special endorsement to cover earthquake damage.

Wear and Tear, Marring, Deterioration:

This is perhaps the most common of all exclusions. It pertains to the normal wear and tear that will inevitably occur to any roof or permanent structure.

Rust, Mold, Wet or Dry Rot:

This type of damage occurs after long exposure to wetness from any source. The idea for this exclusion follows the principle that if the damages were not sudden or accidental, then such damages might have been avoided with proper care to mitigate further damage by making reasonable repairs.

Birds, Vermin, Rodents, Insects or Domestic Animals:

Damages to a roof or the structure caused by any of these critters are not covered. It should be noted, however, that recently a number of claim denials have been challenged and successfully reconsidered and settled concerning raccoons. The insurance company's position is that raccoons are vermin, and thus excluded under most policies. According to the Fire, Casualty & Surety Bulletin (FC&S), an industry newsletter, raccoons are not to be considered vermin. In fact, the dictionary defines raccoons as mammals and not as vermin. Since the term vermin is not clearly defined in the policy, the insured is entitled to the most favorable common usage of the term. So, if you have a claim for damages caused by raccoons, submit your claim with the confidence that this ambiguous term of the policy may lean in your favor.

Ordinance or Law:

An insurance company will usually not cover the cost of enforcement of any law regulating the construction, repair, or demolition of a building or other structure, unless specifically provided for under the policy. Any building code upgrades, for example, are not covered if such are necessary during the course of repairs to a roof or structure unless specifically provided for in a special "endorsement" that the building owner purchased separately and added to his existing insurance policy. If such repairs are necessary, especially in older homes, be sure that you do indeed possess such an endorsement.

Poor Workmanship:

This exclusion will be found under the heading, "Faulty, inadequate or defective . . . . " This could involve planning, zoning, design, citing of a structure, or renovation, remodeling, grading, compaction, materials used in repair, construction, renovation or maintenance of part or all of any property, whether on or off the premises. Any damages that occur as a result of any of these items are probably not covered.

ASBESTOS ABATEMENT

Asbestos can be a significant health hazard to you and your family if not contained or eliminated when identified.

Asbestos was first recognized as a health hazard in 1973 and regulated by the Environmental Protection Agency (EPA) by prohibiting its use in insulation, sound proofing and fire retardation. In the following years, other products containing asbestos were prohibited, such as pipe coverings in 1975, and patching compounds and artificial fireplace materials in 1977. In 1986, additional products containing asbestos were required by the Consumer Product Safety Commission (CPSC) to be labeled as hazardous which, to this day, are components of many households. Some of these products include, but are not limited to:

- asbestos paper
- millboard
- asbestos cement sheet
- furnace and broiler cement
- asbestos wood/coal stove door gaskets
- asbestos laboratory gloves
- asbestos stove mats and iron rests
- furnace duct connectors

In 1989, the EPA issued a ban on the majority of asbestos-based products. The risk associated with asbestos begins with the breakdown of the material itself.

Asbestos is a mineral fiber found in rocks. These fibers are practically immune to destruction, from all sources, including natural processes.

The health risk of asbestos may cause cancer of the lungs and stomach. Because minute fibers of asbestos can literally float in the air, inhaled or ingested fibers can become lodged in tissue, causing health problems even years after exposure.

Asbestos awareness can prevent or restrict the exposure to this hazard. Usually, the products that become soft and easily crumble because of time degradation, have the greatest risk potential.

Identifying asbestos products can be a daunting task for the inexperienced. You should rely on the opinion and survey report of an expert. These professionals, who can be located in your local telephone directory under "asbestos," are trained and experienced in where to look for asbestos, in testing samples, and offering technical advice.

You should be aware of some of the areas in your household which may contain asbestos. If you notice any signs of deterioration or crumbling, consult an expert. Warn your family of any hazardous condition, especially young children. The following is a brief discussion concerning just some of these areas.

Vinyl Sheet Flooring - The backing and adhesive used to secure the flooring can contain asbestos. Fibers can be released when tiles are replaced, dry-scraped, or sanded. You should handle these tiles at a minimum, or avoid contact with these tiles altogether, and simply cover the entire suspected area.

Patching Compounds - Patching compounds manufactured prior to 1977 can contain asbestos. If the compound is still in good condition, it is a wise suggestion to leave the area alone. Remember, just as in asbestos-based flooring, scraping or sanding can release hazardous fibers.

Textured paint - Used on walls and manufactured prior to 1978 can contain asbestos, so extreme caution in renovation or repair should be taken.

Ceilings - Some homes and some large buildings, constructed between 1945 and 1978, may contain degraded asbestos. Materials used were either troweled or sprayed onto ceilings and walls.

If you have a ceiling with crumbling asbestos-containing materials, do not attempt to remove and replace this condition yourself. If it is possible, contact the original contractor to ascertain whether asbestos was used in the ceiling materials.

If you are unable to contact the original contractor, retain the services of an asbestos expert.

Stove and Furnace - Millboard, cement sheets, and paper have been used in wood-burning stove installation. Used as thermal insulation for protecting floors and walls, these materials are highly concentrated in asbestos.

Although cement sheets normally do not release the asbestos fibers unless scraped or sanded, you should still exercise caution. The label on cement sheets may give you an indication of its material makeup and whether it contains asbestos.

Oil and wood furnaces - Could have been insulated with the same hazardous materials. If you upgrade your furnace system, you may disturb the asbestos-based insulation.

Door Gaskets - Furnaces, ovens, and wood or coal stoves can have door gaskets containing asbestos. Normal use of these appliances can cause the asbestos gasket to degrade which causes asbestos fibers to be released. Handle the asbestos material as little as possible, and avoid inhaling any dust particles created by the gasket's wear and tear.

Walls and Pipes - Homes constructed between 1930 and 1950 contained insulation made with asbestos. The asbestos is generally found in walls and ceilings layered behind plaster walls. During renovation and repair, this layer of insulation can be disturbed. It is imperative that if this condition exists, you consult an expert.

Insulation - Insulation containing asbestos and manufactured between 1920 and 1972 was used on and around hot water and steam pipes to "blanket" and protect nearby surfaces. Take extreme caution if this type of insulation shows signs of flaking or degrading.

Appliances - Can pose a health hazard if manufactured prior to the ban on asbestos related parts and components. Parts in some toasters, popcorn poppers, broilers, slow cookers, dishwashers, refrigerators, ovens, ranges, clothes dryers and electric blankets can contain asbestos.

The amount of asbestos used in these products is miniscule, but if you have a suspicion of an older manufactured appliance, allow a repair technician with knowledge of asbestos to check and evaluate your appliance.

Roofing, Shingles and Siding - Asbestos contained in roofing, shingles and siding may not pose a substantial health risk because they are outdoors and not concentrated within the interior of the dwelling. However, if roofing or siding is damaged and the adhesives (portland cement as a binding agent) deteriorate, this could cause a health risk.

If you suspect an area of being asbestos-based, call in an expert to have the material sampled and tested for asbestos exposure and content. This is called a survey and is conducted by companies specializing in asbestos detection.

If the expert you consult to verify the presence of asbestos returns a report that is positive as to the presence of asbestos, consult and retain an asbestos abatement company to remove the hazardous material prior to any restoration effort. Do not vacuum, sweep, or dust suspected asbestos materials.

For more information on asbestos, contact the Consumer Product Safety Commission (CPSC) at 1-800-492-CPSC. A teletypewriter (TTY) for the deaf is available (including Alaska and Hawaii) at 1-800-638-8270, Maryland only (TTY) at 1-800-492-8104.

LEAD-BASED PAINT LAW

If you are an owner of residential property as a primary residence or rental property, you will be subjected to disclosure regulations issued by the federal Environmental Protection Agency (EPA), and the Department of Housing and Urban Development (HUD).

If your home contains lead-based paint, it is your responsibility and a requirement to inform a prospective renter or buyer that the condition exists.

You are also required to provide purchasers and renters with copies of a federally approved lead-based paint hazard pamphlet. Your real estate agent or the EPA should provide you with copies of the pamphlet.

Failure to comply with the rules could subject you to civil penalties up to $10,000, criminal prosecution and a court-imposed fine up to three times any damages incurred by an individual buying or renting your property.

The regulation, as is written, does not affect your homeowners policy of insurance to date, however, it may personally affect you if a renter or purchaser of your home requests that you submit a claim to have the lead-based paint removed and replaced under your existing homeowners policy. Since this is a relatively new law, the submission of claims for coverage under your policy has yet to be clarified.

If you suspect that your home contains lead-based paint, immediately consult your insurance carrier and inquire as to whether or not your insurance policy will honor claims that may arise as a result of the existence of lead-based paint in your house.

Read your policy several times!

SAMPLE OF A REPLACEMENT COST POLICY

NOTE: THIS REPRODUCTION DOES NOT NECESSARILY REFLECT THE COVERAGES ON YOUR OWN HOMEOWNER POLICY.

PAGE 1

SECTION I - COVERAGES

COVERAGE A - DWELLING

1. We cover:
   a. the dwelling used principally as a private residence of the residence premises shown in the Declarations. This includes structures attached to the dwelling;
   b. materials and supplies located on or adjacent to the residence premises for use in the construction, alteration or repair of the dwelling or other structures on the residence premises;
   c. wall-to-wall carpeting attached to the dwelling on the residence premises; and
   d. outdoor antennas.
2. **Dwelling Extension.** We cover other structures on the residence premises, separated from the dwelling by clear space. Structures connected to the dwelling by only a fence, utility line, or similar connection are considered to be other structures.

   We do not cover other structures:
   a. not permanently attached to or otherwise forming a part of the realty;
   b. used in whole or in part for business purposes; or
   c. rented or held for rental to a person not a tenant of the dwelling, unless used solely as a private garage.
3. Except as specifically provided in **SECTION 1 - ADDITIONAL COVERAGES,** Land, we do not cover land, including the land necessary to support any Coverage A property. We do not cover any costs required to replace, rebuild, stabilize, or otherwise restore the land, nor do we cover the costs of repair techniques designed to compensate for or prevent land instability.

COVERAGE B - PERSONAL PROPERTY

1. We cover personal property owned or used by an insured while it is anywhere in the world. This includes structures not permanently attached to or otherwise forming a part of the realty. At your request, we will cover personal property owned by others while the property is on the part of the residence premises occupied exclusively by an insured. At your request, we will also cover personal property owned by a guest or a residence employee, while the property is in any other residence occupied by an insured.

   We cover personal property usually situated at an insured's residence, other than the residence premises, for up to $1,000 or 10% of the Coverage B limit, whichever is greater. This limitation does not apply to personal property in a newly acquired principal residence for the first 30 days after you start moving the property there. If the residence premises is a newly acquired principal residence, personal property in your immediate past principal residence is not subject to this limitation for the first 30 days after the inception of this policy.

   Special Limits of Liability. These limits do not increase the Coverage B limit. The special limit for each of the following categories is the total limit for each loss for all property in that category:
   a. $200 on money, bank notes, coins and medals;
   b. $1,000 on property used or intended for use in a business, including merchandise held as samples or for sale or for delivery after sale, while on the residence premises. This coverage is limited to $250 on such property away from the residence premises.

      Electronic data processing equipment or the recording or storage media used with that equipment is not included under this coverage;
   c. $1,000 on securities, accounts, deeds, evidences of debt, letters of credit, notes other than bank notes, manuscripts, passports, tickets and stamps;
   d. $1,000 on watercraft of all types and outboard motors, including their trailers, furnishings and equipment;
   e. $1,000 on trailers not used with watercraft;
   f. $2,500 for loss by theft of firearms;
   g. $2,500 for loss by theft of silverware or goldware;
   h. $5,000 on electronic data processing equipment and the recording or storage media used with that equipment. There is no coverage for said equipment or media while located away from the residence premises except when said equipment or media are removed from the residence premises for the purpose of repair, servicing or temporary use. An insured student's equipment and media are covered while at a residence away from home; and
   i. $5,000 on any one article and $10,000 in the aggregate for loss by theft of any rug, carpet (except wall-to-wall carpet), tapestry, wall-hanging or other similar article.

      See **SECTION I - ADDITIONAL COVERAGES** for special limits on jewelry, watches, fur garments and garments trimmed with fur, precious and semi-precious stones, gold other than goldware, silver other than silverware, and platinum.
2. **Property Not Covered.** We do not cover:
   a. articles separately described and specifically insured in this or any other insurance;
   b. animals, birds or fish;
   c. any engine or motor propelled vehicle or machine, including the parts, designed for movement on land. We do cover those not licensed for use on public highways which are:
      (1) used solely to service the insured location; or
      (2) designed for assisting the handicapped;
   d. devices or instruments for the recording or reproduction of sound permanently installed in an engine or motor propelled vehicle. We do not cover tapes, wires, records or other mediums that may be used with these devices or instruments while in the vehicle;
   e. aircraft and parts;
   f. property of roomers, boarders, tenants and other residents not related to an insured. We do cover property of roomers, boarders and other residents related to an insured;
   g. property regularly rented or held for rental to others by an insured. This exclusion does not apply to property of an insured in a sleeping room rented to others by an insured;
   h. property rented or held for rental to others away from residence premises;
   i. any citizens band radios, radio telephones, radio transceivers, radio transmitters, radar detectors, antennas and other similar equipment. This exclusion applies only while the property is located in or upon an engine or motor propelled vehicle, whether attached or not;
   j. books of account, abstracts, drawings, card index systems and other records. This exclusion does not apply to file, tape, disc, drum, cell and other magnetic recording or storage media for electronic data processing. We will cover the cost of blank books, cards or other blank material plus the cost of labor you incur for transcribing or copying such records; or
   k. recording or storage media for electronic data processing that cannot be replaced with other of like kind and quality on the current retail market.

COVERAGE C - LOSS OF USE

1. Additional Living Expense. If a Loss Insured causes the residence premises to become uninhabitable, we cover the necessary increase in cost to maintain your standard of living. Payment is for the shortest time required (a) to repair or replace the premises or (b) for your household to settle elsewhere, but not to exceed 12 months. This period of time is not limited by the expiration of this policy.
2. Fair Rental Value. If a Loss Insured causes that part of the residence premises rented to others or held for rental by you to become uninhabitable, we cover its fair rental value. Payment shall be for the shortest time required to repair or replace the part of the premises rented or held for rental but not to exceed 12 months. This period of time is not limited by expiration of this policy. Fair rental value shall not include any expense that does not continue while that part of the residence premises rented or held for rental in uninhabitable.
3. Prohibited Use. If a civil authority prohibits your use of the residence premises because of direct damage to a neighboring premises by a Loss Insured, we cover any resulting Additional Living Expense and Fair Rental Value. Coverage is for a period not exceeding two weeks while use is prohibited.

   We do not cover loss or expense due to cancellation of a lease or agreement.

SECTION I - ADDITIONAL COVERAGES

1. Debris Removal. We will pay the reasonable expenses you incur in the removal of debris of covered property damaged by a Loss Insured. This expense is included in the limit applying to the damaged property.

   We will pay up to $500 in the aggregate for each loss to cover the reasonable expenses you incur in the removal of tree debris from the residence premises when the tree has damaged property covered under Coverage A.

   When the amount payable for the property damage plus the debris removal exceeds the limit for the damaged property, an additional 5% of that limit is available for debris removal expense.
2. **Temporary Repairs.** If damage is caused by a Loss Insured, we will pay the reasonable and necessary cost you incur for temporary repairs to covered property to protect the property from further immediate damage or loss. This coverage does not increase the limit applying to the property being repaired.
3. **Trees, Shrubs and Other Plants.** We cover outdoor trees, shrubs, plants or lawns, on the residence premises, for loss caused by the following: Fire or lightning, Explosion, Riot or civil commotion, Aircraft, Vehicles not owned or operated by a resident of the residence premises, Vandalism or Malicious Mischief or Theft. The limit for this coverage, including the removal of debris, shall not exceed 5% of the limit applying to the dwelling. We will not pay more than $500 for any one outdoor tree, shrub or plant, including debris removal expense. This coverage may increase the limit otherwise applicable. We do not cover property grown for business purposes.
4. **Fire Department Service Charge.** We will pay up to $500 for your liability assumed by contract or agreement for fire department charges. This means charges incurred when the fire department is called to save or protect covered property from a Loss Insured. No deductible applies to this coverage. This coverage may increase the limit otherwise applicable.
5. **Property Removed.** Covered property, while being removed from a premises endangered by a Loss Insured, is covered for any accidental direct physical loss. This coverage also applies to the property for up to 30 days while removed. We will also pay for reasonable expenses incurred by you for the removal and return of the covered property. This coverage does not increase the limit applying to the property being removed.
6. **Credit Card, Bank Fund Transfer Card, Forgery and Counterfeit Money.**
   a. We will pay up to $1,000 for:
      (1) the legal obligation of an insured to pay because of the theft or unauthorized use of credit cards and bank fund transfer cards issued to or registered in an insured's name. If an insured has not complied with all terms and conditions under which the cards are issued, we do not cover use by an insured or anyone else;
      (2) loss to an insured caused by forgery or alteration of any check or negotiable instrument; and
      (3) loss to an insured through acceptance in good faith of counterfeit United States or Canadian paper currency.

      No deductible applies to this coverage.

      We will not pay more than the limit stated above for forgery or alteration committed by any one person. This limit applies when the forgery or alteration involves one or more instrument in the same loss.
   b. We do not cover loss arising out of business pursuits or dishonesty of an insured.
   c. Defense:
      (1) We may make any investigation and settle any claim or suit that we decide is appropriate. Our obligation to defend claims or suits ends when the amount we pay for the loss equals our limit of liability.
      (2) If claim is made or a suit is brought against an insured for liability under the Credit Card or Bank Fund Transfer Card coverage, we will provide a defense. This defense is at our expense by counsel of our choice.
      (3) We have the option to defend at our expense an insured or insured's bank against any suit for the enforcement of payment under the Forgery coverage.
7. **Power Interruption.** We cover accidental direct physical loss caused directly or indirectly by a change of temperature which results from power interruption that takes place on the residence premises. The power interruption must be caused by a Loss Insured occurring on the residence premises. The power lines off the residence premises must remain energized. This coverage does not increase the limit applying to the damaged property.
8. **Refrigerated Products.** Coverage B is extended to cover the contents of deep freeze or refrigerated units on the residence premises for loss due to power failure or mechanical failure. If mechanical failure or power failure is known to you, all reasonable means must be used to protect the property insured from further damage or this coverage is void. Power failure or mechanical failure shall not include:
   a. removal of a plug from an electrical outlet; or
   b. turning off an electrical switch unless caused by a Loss Insured.

   This coverage does not increase the limit applying to the damaged property.
9. **Arson Reward.** We will pay $1,000 for information which leads to an arson conviction in connection with a fire loss to property covered by this policy. This coverage may increase the limit otherwise applicable. However, the $1,000 limit shall not be increased regardless of the number of persons providing information.
10. **Jewelry and Furs.** Jewelry, watches, fur garments and garments trimmed with fur, precious and semi-precious stones, gold other than goldware, silver other than silverware, and platinum are insured for accidental direct physical loss or damage.

    We do not cover loss or damage caused by mechanical breakdown, wear and tear, gradual deterioration, insects, vermin, inherent vice, or seizure or destruction under quarantine or customs regulations.

    In addition to limitations and exclusions otherwise applicable, the following also apply:
    a. our limit for loss by any Coverage B peril except theft shall be the limit stated in the Declarations for Coverage B, plus $2,500; and
    b. our limit for loss by theft and any covered peril, except those in item a., shall be $1,500 on any one article and $2,500 in the aggregate.
11. **Land.** If a single event results in both a Loss Insured to the insured dwelling, other than the breakage of glass or safety glazing material, and a loss of land stability, we will pay up to $10,000 as an additional amount of insurance for repair costs associated with the land. This includes the costs required to replace, rebuild, stabilize or otherwise restore the land. This Additional Coverage applies only to the land necessary to support that part of the insured dwelling sustaining the Loss Insured.
12. **Volcanic Action.** We cover direct physical loss to a covered building or covered property contained in a building resulting from the eruption of a volcano when the loss is directly and immediately caused by:
    a. volcanic blast or airborne shock waves;
    b. ash, dust or particulate matter; or
    c. lava flow.

    We will also pay for the removal of that ash, dust or particulate matter which has caused direct physical loss to a covered building or covered property contained in a building.

    One or more volcanic eruptions that occur within a 72 hour period shall be considered one volcanic eruption.

    This coverage does not increase the limit applying to the damaged property.
13. **Collapse.** We insure for direct physical loss to covered property involving collapse of a building or any part of a building caused only by one or more of the following:
    a. perils described in SECTION I - LOSSES INSURED, COVERAGE B - PERSONAL PROPERTY. These perils apply to covered building and personal property for loss insured by this Additional Coverage;
    b. hidden decay;
    c. hidden insect or vermin damage;
    d. weight of contents, equipment, animals or people;
    e. weight of ice, snow, sleet or rain which collects on a roof; or
    f. use of defective material or methods in construction, remodeling or renovation if the collapse occurs during the course of construction, remodeling or renovation.

    Loss to an awning, fence, patio, pavement, swimming pool, underground pipe, flue, drain, cesspool, septic tank, foundation, retaining wall, bulkhead, pier, wharf or dock is not included under items b., c., d., e., and f. unless the loss is a direct result of the collapse of a building.

    Collapse does not include settling, cracking, shrinking, bulging or expansion.

SAMPLE OF A REPLACEMENT COST POLICY

NOTE: THIS REPRODUCTION DOES NOT NECESSARILY REFLECT THE COVERAGES ON YOUR OWN HOMEOWNER POLICY.

PAGE 2

This coverage does not increase the limit applying to the damaged property.

14. **Locks.** We will pay the reasonable expenses you incur to re-key locks on exterior doors of the dwelling located on the residence premises, when the keys to those locks are a part of a covered theft loss.

    No deductible applies to this coverage.

15. **Temporary Living Expense Allowance.** If the residence premises becomes uninhabitable because of a loss caused by earthquake, landslide, flood or volcanic explosion, or if a civil authority prohibits your use of the residence premises because an earthquake, landslide, flood or volcanic explosion has occurred, we will pay up to $2,000 to cover the necessary increase in cost which you incur to maintain your standard of living.

    The SECTION I - LOSSES NOT INSURED references to earthquake, landslide, flood and volcanic explosion do not apply to this Additional Coverage.

    This coverage is excess over any other valid and collectible insurance which is in force at the time of the loss.

    No deductible applies to this coverage.

INFLATION COVERAGE

The limits of liability shown in the Declarations for Coverages A and B will be increased at the same rate as the increase in the Inflation Coverage Index shown in the Declarations.

To find the limits on a given date:

1. divide the Index on that date by the Index as of the effective date of this Inflation Coverage provision; then
2. multiply the resulting factor by the limits of liability for Coverages A and B separately.

The limits of liability will not be reduced to less than the amounts shown in the Declarations.

If during the term of this policy the Coverage A limit of liability is changed at your request, the effective date of this Inflation Coverage provision is changed to coincide with the effective date of such change.

GUARANTEED EXTRA COVERAGE

We will settle covered losses to the dwelling under Coverage A and other building structures under Dwelling Extension at replacement cost without regard to the limit of liability, subject to the Loss Settlement provisions in SECTION I - CONDITIONS.

Except as specifically provided in SECTION I - ADDITIONAL COVERAGES, Land, we will not pay for land, including the land necessary to support any Coverage A property, or any costs required to replace, rebuild, stabilize, or otherwise restore the land, nor will we pay the costs of repair techniques designed to compensate for or prevent land instability.

Report Increased Values.

You must notify us within 90 days of the start of any new building valued at $5,000 or more or any additions to or remodeling of buildings which increase their values by $5,000 or more and pay any additional premium due for the increase in value. If you fail to notify us within 90 days, our payment will not exceed the limit of liability applying to the building.

See SECTION I - CONDITIONS, Loss Settlement for additional provisions.

SECTION I - LOSSES INSURED

COVERAGE A - DWELLING

We insure for accidental direct physical loss to the property described in Coverage A, except as provided in SECTION I - LOSSES NOT INSURED.

COVERAGE B - PERSONAL PROPERTY

We insure for accidental direct physical loss to property described in Coverage B caused by the following perils, except as provided in SECTION I - LOSSES NOT INSURED:

1. **Fire or lightning.**
2. **Windstorm or hail.** This peril does not include loss to property contained in a building caused by rain, snow, sleet, sand or dust. This limitation does not apply when the direct force of wind or hail damages the building causing an opening in a roof or wall and the rain, snow, sleet, sand or dust enters through this opening.
3. **Explosion.**
4. **Riot or civil commotion.**
5. **Aircraft,** including self-propelled missiles and spacecraft.
6. **Vehicles.**
7. **Smoke,** meaning sudden and accidental damage from smoke.
8. **Vandalism or malicious mischief**, meaning only willful and malicious damage to or destruction of property.
9. **Theft,** including attempted theft and loss of property from a known location when it is probable that the property has been stolen.

   This peril does not include:

   a. loss of a precious or semi-precious stone from its setting;

   b. loss caused by theft:

   (1) committed by an insured or by any other person regularly residing on the insured location. Property of a student who is an insured is covered while located at a residence away from home, if the theft is committed by a person who is not an insured;

   (2) in or to a dwelling under construction or of materials and supplies for use in the construction until the dwelling is completed and occupied; or

   (3) from the part of a residence premises rented to others:

   (a) caused by a tenant, members of the tenant's household, or the tenant's employees;

   (b) of money, bank notes, bullion, gold, goldware, silver, silverware, pewterware, platinum, coins and medals;

   (c) of securities, checks, cashier's checks, traveler's checks, money orders and other negotiable instruments, accounts, deeds, evidences of debt, letters of credit, notes other than bank notes, manuscripts, passports, tickets and stamps; or

   (d) of jewelry, watches, fur garments and garments trimmed with fur, precious and semi-precious stones.

   c. loss caused by theft that occurs away from the residence premises of:

   (1) property while at any other residence owned, rented to, or occupied by an insured, except while an insured is temporarily residing there. Property of a student who is an insured is covered while at a residence away from home;

   (2) watercraft of all types, including their furnishings, equipment and outboard motors; or

   (3) trailers and campers designed to be pulled by or carried on a vehicle.

   If the residence premises is a newly acquired principal residence, property in the immediate past principal residence shall not be considered property away from the residence premises for the first 30 days after the inception of this policy.

10. **Falling objects.** This peril does not include loss to property contained in a building unless the roof or an exterior wall of the building is first damaged by a falling object. Damage to the falling object itself is not included.
11. Weight of ice, snow or sleet which causes damage to property contained in a building.
12. **Sudden and accidental discharge or overflow** of water or steam from within a plumbing, heating, air conditioning or automatic fire protective sprinkler system, or from within a household appliance.

    This peril does not include loss:

    a. to the system or appliance from which the water or steam escaped;

    b. caused by or resulting from freezing;

    c. caused by or resulting from water from outside the plumbing system that enters through sewers or drains, or water which enters into and overflows from within a sump pump, sump pump well or other type system designed to remove subsurface water which is drained from the foundation area; or

    d. caused by or resulting from continuous or repeated seepage or leakage of water or steam which occurs over a period of time and results in deterioration, corrosion, rust, mold, or wet or dry rot.

13. **Sudden and accidental tearing asunder, cracking, burning or bulging** of a steam or hot water heating system, an air conditioning or automatic fire protective sprinkler system, or an appliance for heating water.

    This peril does not include loss:

    a. caused by or resulting from freezing; or

    b. caused by or resulting from continuous or repeated seepage or leakage of water or steam which occurs over a period of time and results in deterioration, corrosion, rust, mold, or wet or dry rot.

14. **Freezing** of a plumbing, heating, air conditioning or automatic fire protective sprinkler system, or of a household appliance.

    This peril does not include loss on the residence premises while the dwelling is vacant, unoccupied or being constructed, unless you have used reasonable care to:

    a. maintain heating in the building; or

    b. shut off the water supply and drain the system and appliances of water.

15. **Sudden and accidental damage** to electrical appliances, devices, fixtures and wiring from an increase or decrease of artificially generated electrical current. We will pay up to $1,000 under this peril for each damaged item described above.
16. **Breakage of glass,** meaning damage to personal property caused by breakage of glass which is a part of a building on the residence premises. There is no coverage for loss or damage to the glass.

SECTION I - LOSSES NOT INSURED

1. We do not insure for any loss to the property described in Coverage A which is caused by one or more of the items below, regardless of whether the loss occurs suddenly or gradually, involves isolated or widespread damage, arises from natural or external forces, or occurs as a result of any combination of these:

   a. collapse, except as specifically provided in **SECTION I - ADDITIONAL COVERAGES, Collapse;**

   b. freezing of a plumbing, heating, air conditioning or automatic fire protective sprinkler system, or of a household appliance, or by discharge, leakage or overflow from within the system or appliance caused by freezing. This exclusion only applies while the dwelling is vacant, unoccupied or being constructed. This exclusion does not apply if you have used reasonable care to:

   (1) maintain heat in the building; or

   (2) shut off the water supply and drain the system and appliances of water;

   c. freezing, thawing, pressure or weight of water or ice, whether driven by wind or not, to a fence, pavement, patio, swimming pool, foundation, retaining wall, bulkhead, pier, wharf or dock;

   d. theft in or to a dwelling under construction, or of materials and supplies for use in the construction, until the dwelling is completed and occupied;

   e. vandalism or malicious mischief or breakage of glass and safety glazing materials if the dwelling has been vacant for more than 30 consecutive days immediately before the loss. A dwelling being constructed is not considered vacant;

   f. continuous or repeated seepage or leakage of water or steam from a:

   (1) heating, air conditioning or automatic fire protective sprinkler system;

   (2) household appliance; or

   (3) plumbing system, including from, within or around any shower stall, shower bath, tub installation, or other plumbing fixture, including their walls, ceilings or floors;

   which occurs over a period of time and result in deterioration, corrosion, rust, mold or wet or dry rot. If loss to covered property is caused by water or steam not otherwise excluded, we will cover the cost of tearing out and replacing any part of the building necessary to repair the system or appliance. we do not cover loss to the system or appliance from which the water or steam escaped;

   g. wear, tear, marring, scratching, deterioration, inherent vice, latent deft or mechanical breakdown;

   h. corrosion, electrolysis or rust;

   i. mold, or wet or dry rot;

   j. contamination;

   k. smog, smoke from agricultural smudging or industrial operations;

   l. settling, cracking, shrinking, bulging, or expansion of pavements, patios, foundation, walls, floors, roofs or ceilings; or

   m. birds, vermin, rodents, insects, or domestic animals. We do cover the breakage of glass or safety glazing material which is a part of a building, when caused by birds, vermin, rodents, insects or domestic animals.

   However, we do insure for any resulting loss from items a. through m. unless the resulting loss itself a Loss Not Insured by this Section.

2. We do not insure under any coverage for any loss which would not have occurred in the absence of one or more of the following excluded events. We do not insure for such loss regardless of: (a) the cause of the excluded event; or (b) other causes of the loss; or (c) whether other causes acted concurrently or in any sequence with the excluded event to produce the loss; or (d) whether the event occurs suddenly or gradually, involves isolated or widespread damage, arises from natural or external forces, or occurs as a result of any combination of these:

   a. **Earthquake.**

   We do insure for any direct loss by fire, explosion other than explosion of a volcano, theft, or breakage of glass or safety glazing materials which are part of the dwelling resulting from earthquake, provided the resulting loss is itself a Loss Insured.

SAMPLE OF A REPLACEMENT COST POLICY

NOTE: THIS REPRODUCTION DOES NOT NECESSARILY REFLECT THE COVERAGES ON YOUR OWN HOMEOWNER POLICY.

PAGE 3

b. **Nuclear Hazard**, meaning any nuclear reaction, radiation, or radioactive contamination, all whether controlled or uncontrolled or however caused, or any consequence of any of these. Loss caused by the nuclear hazard shall not be considered loss caused by fire, explosion, or smoke. However, we do insure for direct loss by fire resulting from the nuclear hazard.

3. We do not insure under any coverage for any loss which is caused by one or more of the items below, regardless of whether the event occurs suddenly or gradually, involves isolated or widespread damage, arises from natural or external forces, or occurs as a result of any combination of these:
   a. **Ordinance or Law**, meaning enforcement of any ordinance or law regulating the construction, repair or demolition of a building or other structure, unless specifically provided under this policy.
   b. **Earth Movement**, meaning the sinking, rising, shifting, expanding or contracting of earth, all whether combine with water or not. Earth movement includes but is not limited to landslide, mudflow, sinkhole, subsidence and erosion. Earth movement also includes volcanic explosion or lava flow, except as specifically provided in SECTION I - ADDITIONAL COVERAGES, Volcanic Action.

      We do insure for any direct loss by fire, explosion other than explosion of a volcano, theft, or breakage of glass or safety glazing materials which are part of the dwelling resulting from earth movement, provided the resulting loss is itself a Loss Insured.
   c. **Water Damage**, meaning:
      (1) flood, surface water, waves, tidal water, overflow of a body of water, or spray from any of these, all whether driven by wind or not;
      (2) water from outside the plumbing system that enters through sewers or drains, or water which enters into and overflows from within a sump pump, sump pump well or any other system designed to remove subsurface water which is drained from the foundation area; or
      (3) natural water below the surface of the ground, including water which exerts pressure on, or seeps or leaks through a building, sidewalk, driveway, foundation, swimming pool or other structure.

      However, we do not insure for any direct loss by fire, explosion or theft resulting from water damage, provided the resulting loss is itself a Loss Insured.
   d. **Neglect**, meaning neglect of the insured to use all reasonable means to save and preserve property at and after the time of a loss, or when property is endangered.
   e. **War**, including any undeclared war, civil war, insurrection, rebellion, revolution, warlike act by a military force or military personnel, destruction or seizure or use for a military purpose, and including any consequence of any of these. Discharge of a nuclear weapon shall be deemed a warlike act even if accidental.
4. We do not insure for loss described in paragraphs 1., 2. and 3 immediately above regardless of whether one or more of the following: (a) directly or indirectly cause, contribute to or aggravate the loss; or (b) occur before, at the same time, or after the loss or any other cause of the loss:
   a. conduct, act, failure to act, or decision of any person, group, organization or governmental body whether intentional, wrongful, negligent, or without fault; or
   b. defect, weakness, inadequacy, fault or unsoundness in
      (1) planning, zoning, development, surveying, sitting;
      (2) design, specifications, workmanship, construction, grading, compaction;
      (3) materials used in construction or repair; or
      (4) maintenance;

   of any property (including land, structures, or improvements of any kind) whether on or off the residence premises.

   However, we do insure for any resulting loss from items a. and b. unless the resulting loss is itself a Loss Not Insured by this Section.
5. We do not insure under any coverage for any loss consisting of the items in paragraphs 1., 2., 3 or 4. This exclusion does not apply if the loss is caused by a peril which is not otherwise excluded.

SECTION I - CONDITIONS

1. **Insurable Interest and Limit of Liability.** Even if more than one person has an insurable interest in the property covered, we shall not be liable:
   a. to the insured for an amount greater than the insured's interest; or
   b. for more than the applicable limit of liability.
2. **Your Duties After Loss.** After a loss to which this insurance may apply, you shall see that the following duties are performed:
   a. give immediate notice to us or our agent. Also notify the police if the loss is caused by theft. Also notify the credit card company or bank if the loss involves a credit card or bank fund transfer card;
   b. protect the property from further damage or loss, make reasonable and necessary temporary repairs required to protect the property, keep an accurate record of repair expenditures;
   c. prepare an inventory of damaged or stolen personal property. Show in detail the quantity, description, actual cash value and amount of loss. Attach to the inventory all bills, receipts and related documents that substantiate the figures in the inventory;
   d. as often as we reasonably require:
      (1) exhibit the damaged property;
      (2) provide us with records and documents we request and permit us to make copies;
      (3) submit to and subscribe, while not in the presence of any other insured:
         (a) statements; and
         (b) examinations under oath; and
      (4) produce employees, members of the insured's household or others for examination under oath to the extent it is within insured's power to do so; and
   e. submit to us, within 60 days after the loss, your signed, sworn proof of loss which sets forth, to the best of your knowledge and belief:
      (1) the time and cause of loss;
      (2) interest of the insured and all others in the property involved and all encumbrances on the property;
      (3) other insurance which may cover the loss;
      (4) changes in title or occupancy of the property during the term of this policy;
      (5) specifications of any damaged building and detailed estimates for repair of the damage;
      (6) an inventory of damaged or stolen personal property described in 2.c;
      (7) receipts for additional living expenses incurred and records supporting the fair rental value loss;
      (8) evidence or affidavit supporting a claim under the Credit Card, Bank Fund Transfer Card, Forgery and Counterfeit Money coverage, stating the amount and cause of loss.
3. **Loss Settlement.** Covered property losses are settled as follows:
   a. We will pay actual cash value at the time of loss for:
      (1) antiques, fine arts, painting, statuary and similar articles which by their inherent nature cannot be replaced with new articles;
      (2) articles whose age or history contribute substantially to their value including, but not limited to, memorabilia, souvenirs and collectors items;
      (3) property not useful for its intended purpose.

      However, we will not pay an amount exceeding the applicable limit of liability or an amount exceeding that necessary to repair or replace the property.
   b. We will pay the cost to repair or replace other personal property, carpeting, domestic appliances, awnings and outdoor antennas whether or not attached to buildings, subject to the following:
      (1) loss to property not repaired or replaced within one year after the loss will be settled on an actual cash value basis;
      (2) we will not pay an amount exceeding the smallest of the following:
         (a) replacement cost at the time of loss;
         (b) the full cost of repair;
         (c) any special limit of liability described in the policy; or
         (d) any applicable Coverage A or Coverage B limit of liability.
   c. We will pay the cost to repair or replace buildings under Coverage A and other structures under Dwelling Extension, subject to the following:
      (1) until actual repair or replacement is completed, we will pay the actual cash value of the damage to the buildings or other structures, up to the policy limits, not to exceed the replacement cost of the damaged part of the building or other structures, for equivalent construction and use on the same premises;
      (2) you must make claim within 180 days after the loss for any additional payment on a replacement cost basis.

         Any additional payment is limited to that amount you actually and necessarily spend to repair or replace the damaged buildings or other structures with equivalent construction and for equivalent use on the same premises;
      (3) we will not pay more than the $10,000 limit on land as provided in SECTION I - ADDITIONAL COVERAGES; and
      (4) we will not pay for increased costs resulting from enforcement of any ordinance or law regulating the construction, repair, or demolition of a building or other structure, unless specifically provided under this policy.
4. Loss to a Pair or Set. In case of loss to a pair or set, we may elect to:
   a. repair or replace any part to restore the pair or set to its value before the loss; or
   b. pay the difference between actual cash value of the property before and after the loss.
5. **Glass Replacement.** Loss for damage to glass caused by a Loss Insured shall be settled on the basis of replacement with safety glazing materials when required by ordinance or law.
6. **Appraisal.** If you and we fail to agree on the amount of loss, either one can demand that the amount of the loss be set by appraisal. If either makes a written demand for appraisal, each shall select a competent, independent appraiser. Each shall notify the other of the appraiser's identity within 20 days of receipt of the written demand. The two appraisers shall then select a competent, impartial umpire. If the two appraisers are unable to agree upon an umpire within 15 days, you or we can ask a judge of a court of record in the state where the residence premises is located to select an umpire. The appraisers shall then set the amount of the loss. If the appraisers submit a written report of an agreement to us, the amount agreed upon shall be the amount of the loss. If the appraisers fail to agree within a reasonable time, they shall submit their differences to the umpire. Written agreement signed by any two of these three shall set the amount of the loss. Each appraiser shall be paid by the party selecting that appraiser. Other expenses of the appraisal and the compensation of the umpire shall be paid equally by you and us.
7. **Other Insurance.** If a loss covered by this policy is also covered by other insurance, we will pay only our share of the loss. Our share is the proportion of the loss that the applicable limit under this policy bears to the total amount of insurance covering the loss.
8. **Suit Against Us.** No action shall be brought unless there has been compliance with the policy provisions. The action must be started within one year after the date of loss or damage.
9. **Our Option.** We may repair or replace any part of the property damaged or stolen with equivalent property. Any property we pay for or replace becomes our property.
10. **Loss Payment.** We will adjust all losses with you. We will pay you unless some other person is named in the policy or is legally entitled to receive payment. Loss will be payable 30 days after we receive your proof of loss and:
    a. reach agreement with you;
    b. there is an entry of a final judgment; or
    c. there is a filing of an appraisal award with us.
11. **Abandonment of Property.** We need not accept any property abandoned by an insured.
12. **Mortgage Clause.** The word "mortgagee" includes trustee:
    a. If a mortgagee is named in this policy, any loss payable under Coverage A shall be paid to the mortgagee and you, as interests appear. If more than one mortgagee is named, the order of payment shall be the same as the order of precedence of the mortgages.
    b. If we deny your claim, that denial shall not apply to a valid claim of the mortgagee, if the mortgagee:
       (1) notifies us of any change in ownership, occupancy or substantial change in risk of which the mortgagee is aware;
       (2) pays any premium due under this policy on demand if you have neglected to pay the premium; or
       (3) submits a signed, sworn statement of loss within 60 days after receiving notice from us of your failure to do so. Policy conditions relating to Appraisal, Suit Against Us and Loss Payment apply to the mortgagee.
    c. If this policy is canceled by us, the mortgagee shall be notified at least 10 days before the date cancellation takes effect.
    d. If we pay the mortgagee for any loss and deny payment to you:
       (1) we are subrogated to all the rights of the mortgagee granted under the mortgage on the property; or
       (2) at our option, we may pay to the mortgagee the whole principal on the mortgage plus any accrued interest. In this event, we shall receive a full assignment and transfer of the mortgage and all securities held as collateral to the mortgage debt.
    e. Subrogation shall not impair the right of the mortgagee to recover the full amount of the mortgagee's claim.
13. **No Benefit to Bailee.** We will not recognize as assignment or grant coverage for the benefit of a person or organization holding, storing or transporting property for a fee. This applies regardless of any other provision of this policy.
14. **Intentional Acts.** If you or any person insured under this policy causes or procures a loss to property covered under this policy for the purpose of obtaining insurance benefits, then this policy is void and we will not pay you or any other insured for the loss.

SAMPLE OF A REPLACEMENT COST POLICY
NOTE: THIS REPRODUCTION <u>DOES NOT NECESSARILY</u> REFLECT THE COVERAGES ON YOUR OWN HOMEOWNER POLICY.
PAGE 4

SECTION II - LIABILITY COVERAGES

COVERAGE L - PERSONAL LIABILITY

If a claim is made or a suit is brought again an insured for damages because of bodily injury or property damage to which this coverage applies, caused by an occurrence, we will:

1. pay up to our limit of liability for the damages for which the insured is legally liable; and
2. provide a defense at our expense by counsel of our choice. We may make any investigation and settle any claim or suit that we decide is appropriate. Our obligation to defend any claim or suit ends when the amount we pay for damages, to effect settlement or satisfy a judgment result from the occurrence, equals our limit of liability.

COVERAGE M - MEDICAL PAYMENTS TO OTHERS

We will pay the necessary medical expenses incurred or medically ascertained within three years from the date of any accident causing bodily injury. Medical expenses means reasonable charges for medical, surgical, x-ray, dental, ambulance, hospital, professional nursing, prosthetic devices and funeral services. This coverage applies only:

1. to a person on the insured location with the permission of an insured;
2. to a person off the insured location, if the bodily injury:
   a. arises out of a condition on the insured location or the ways immediately adjoining;
   b. is caused by the activities of an insured;
   c. is caused by a residence employee in the course of the residence employee's employment by an insured; or
   d. is caused by an animal owned by or in the care of any insured; or
3. to a residence employee if the occurrence causing bodily injury occurs off the insured location and arises out of or in the course of the residence employee's employment by an insured.

SECTION II - ADDITIONAL COVERAGES

We cover the following in addition to the limits of liability:

1. Claim Expenses. We pay:
   a. expenses we incur and costs taxed against an insured in suits we defend;
   b. premiums on bonds required in suits we defend, but not for bond amounts greater than the Coverage L limit. We are not obligated to apply for or furnish any bond;
   c. reasonable expenses as insured incurs at our request. This includes actual loss of earnings (but not loss of other income) up to $100 per day for aiding us in the investigation or defense of claims or suits;
   d. prejudgment interest awarded against the insured on that part of the judgment we pay; and
   e. interest on the entire judgment which accrues after entry of the judgment and before we pay or tender, or deposit in court that part of the judgment which does not exceed the limit of liability that applies.
2. First Aid Expenses. We will pay expenses for first aid to others incurred by an insured for bodily injury covered under this policy. We will not pay for first aid to you or any other insured.
3. Damage to Property of Others:
   a. We will pay for property damage to property of others caused by an insured.
   b. We will not pay more than the smallest of the following amounts:
      (1) replacement cost at the time of loss;
      (2) full cost of repair; or
      (3) $500 in any one occurrence.
   c. We will not pay for property damage:
      (1) if insurance is otherwise provided in this policy;
      (2) caused intentionally by an insured who is 13 years of age or older;
      (3) to property, other than a rented golf cart, owned by or rented to an insured, a tenant of an insured, or a resident in your household; or
      (4) arising out of:
         (a) business pursuits;
         (b) any act or omission in connection with a premises an insured owns, rents or controls, other than the insured location; or
         (c) the ownership, maintenance, or use of a motor vehicle, aircraft, or watercraft, including airboat, air cushion, personal watercraft, sail board or similar type watercraft.

SECTION II - EXCLUSIONS

Coverage L and Coverage M do not apply to:

a. bodily injury or property damage:
   (1) which is either expected or intended by an insured; or
   (2) to any person or property which is the result of willful and malicious acts of an insured;
b. bodily injury or property damage arising out of business pursuits of any insured or the rental or holding for rental of any part of any premises by an insured. This exclusion does not apply:
   (1) to activities which are ordinarily incident to non-business pursuits;
   (2) with respect to Coverage L to the occasional or part-time business pursuits of an insured who is under 19 years of age;
   (3) to the rental or holding for rental of a residence of yours:
      (a) on an occasional basis for the exclusive use of a residence;
      (b) in part, unless intended for use as a residence by more than two roomers or boarders; or
      (c) in part, as an office, school, studio or private garage;
   (4) when the dwelling in the residence premises is a two, three or four-family dwelling and you occupy one part and rent or hold for rental the other parts; or
   (5) to farm land (without buildings) not in excess of 500 acres, rented or held for rental to others;
c. bodily injury or property damage arising out of the rendering or failing to render professional services;
d. bodily injury or property damage arising out of any premises owned or rented to any insured which is not an insured location. This exclusion does not apply to bodily injury to a residence employee arising out of and in the course of the residence employee's employment by an insured;
e. bodily injury or property damage arising out of the ownership, maintenance, use, loading or unloading of:
   (1) an aircraft;
   (2) a motor vehicle owned or operated by or rented or loan to any insured; or
   (3) a watercraft:
      (a) owned by or rented to any insured if it has inboard or inboard-outdrive motor power of more than 50 horsepower;
      (b) owned by or rented to any insured if it is a sailing vessel, with or without auxiliary power, 26 feet or more in overall length;
      (c) powered by one or more outboard motors with more than 25 total horsepower owned by any insured;
      (d) designated as an airboat, air cushion, or similar type of craft; or
      (e) owned by an insured which is a personal watercraft using a water jet pump powered by an infernal combustion engine as the primary source of propulsion.
   This exclusion does not apply to bodily injury to a residence employee arising out of and in the course of the residence employee's employment by an insured. Exclusion e.(3) does not apply while the watercraft is on the residence premises;
f. bodily injury or property damage arising out of:
   (1) the entrustment by any insured to any person;
   (2) the supervision by any insured of any person;
   (3) any liability statutorily imposed on any insured; or
   (4) any liability assumed through an unwritten or written agreement by any insured;
   with regard to the ownership, maintenance or use of any aircraft, watercraft, or motor vehicle (or any other motorized land conveyance) which is not covered under Section II of this policy;
g. bodily injury or property damage caused directly or indirectly by war, including undeclared war, or any warlike act including destruction or seizure or use for a military purpose, or any consequence of these.
   Discharge of a nuclear weapon shall be deemed warlike even if accidental;
h. bodily injury to you or any insured within the meaning of part a. or b. of the definition of insured.
   This exclusion also applies to any claim made or suit brought against any insured to share damages with or repay someone else who may be obligated to pay damages because of the bodily injury;
i. any claim made or suit brought against any insured by:
   (1) any person who is in the care of any insured because of child care services provided by or at the direction of:
      (a) any insured;
      (b) any employee of any insured; or
      (c) any other person actually or apparently acting on behalf of any insured; or
   (2) any person who makes a claim because of bodily injury to any person who is in the care of any insured because of child care services provided by or at the direction of:
      (a) any insured;
      (b) any employee of any insured; or
      (c) any other person actually or apparently acting on behalf of any insured.
   This exclusion does not apply to the occasional child care services provided by any insured, or to the part-time child care services provided by any insured who is under 19 years of age; or
j. bodily injury or property damage arising out of any insured's participation in, or preparation or practice for any prearranged or organized race, speed or demolition contest, or similar competition involving a motorized land vehicle or motorized watercraft. This exclusion does not apply to a sailing vessel less than 26 feet in overall length with or without auxiliary power.

2. Coverage L does not apply to:
   a. liability:
      (1) for your share of any loss assessment charged against all members of any association of property owners; or
      (2) assumed under any unwritten contract or agreement, or by contract or agreement in connection with a business of the insured;
   b. property damage to property owned by any insured;
   c. property damage to property rented to, occupied or used by or in the care of any insured. This exclusion does not apply to property damage caused by fire, smoke or explosion;
   d. bodily injury to a person eligible to receive any benefits required to be provided or voluntarily provided by an insured under a workers' compensation, non-occupational disability, or occupational disease law;
   e. bodily injury or property damage for which an insured under this policy is also an insured under a nuclear energy liability policy or would be an insured but for its termination upon exhaustion of its limit of liability. A nuclear energy liability policy is a policy issued by Nuclear Energy Liability Underwriters, Nuclear Insurance Association of Canada, or any of their successors.

3. Coverage M does not apply to bodily injury:
   a. to a residence employee if it occurs off the insured location and does not arise out of or in the course of the residence employee's employment by an insured;
   b. to a person eligible to receive any benefits required to be provided or voluntarily provided under any workers' compensation, non-occupation disability or occupational disease law;
   c. from nuclear reaction, radiation or radioactive contamination, all whether controlled or uncontrolled or however caused, or any consequence of any of these;
   d. to a person other than a residence employee of an insured, regularly residing on any part of the insured location.

SAMPLE OF A REPLACEMENT COST POLICY

NOTE: THIS REPRODUCTION DOES NOT NECESSARILY REFLECT THE COVERAGES ON YOUR OWN HOMEOWNER POLICY.

PAGE 5

SECTION II - CONDITIONS

1. **Limit of Liability.** The Coverage L limit is shown in the Declarations. This is our limit for all damages from each occurrence regardless of the number of insureds, claims made or persons injured.

   The Coverage M limit is shown in the Declarations. This is our limit for all medical expense for bodily injury to one person as the result of one accident.
2. **Severability of Insurance.** This insurance applies separately to each insured. This condition shall not increase our limit of liability for any one occurrence.
3. **Duties After Loss.** In case of an accident or occurrence, the insured shall perform the following duties that apply. You shall cooperate with us in seeing that these duties are performed:
   a. give written notice to us or our agent as soon as practicable; which sets forth:
      (1) the identity of this policy and insured;
      (2) reasonably available information on the time, place and circumstances of the accident or occurrence; and
      (3) names and addresses of any claimants and available witnesses;
   b. immediately forward to us every notice, demand, summons or other process relating to the accident or occurrence;
   c. at our request, assist in
      (1) making settlement;
      (2) the enforcement of any right of contribution or indemnity against a person or organization who may be liable to an insured;
      (3) the conduct of suits and attend hearings and trials; and
      (4) securing and giving evidence and obtaining the attendance of witnesses;
   d. under the coverage - Damage to Property of Others:
      (1) submit a sworn statement of loss to us within 60 days after the loss; and
      (2) exhibit the damaged property if within the insured's control; and
   e. the insured shall not, except at the insured's own cost, voluntarily make payments, assume obligations to incur expenses. This does not apply to expense for first aid to others at the time of the bodily injury.
4. **Duties of an Injured Person** - Coverage M. The injured person, or, when appropriate, someone acting on behalf of that person, shall:
   a. give us written proof of claim, under oath if required, as soon as practicable;
   b. execute authorization to allow us to obtain copies of medical reports and records; and
   c. submit to physical examination by a physician selected by us when and as often as we reasonably require.
5. **Payment of Claim** - Coverage M. Payment under this coverage is not an admission of liability by an insured or us.
6. **Suit Against Us.** No one shall have the right to join us as a party to an action against an insured. Further, no action with respect to Coverage L shall be brought against us until the obligation of the insured has been determined by final judgment or agreement signed by us.
7. **Bankruptcy of any Insured**. Bankruptcy or insolvency of an insured shall not relieve us of our obligation under this policy.
8. **Other Insurance - Coverage L.** This insurance is excess over any other valid and collectible insurance except insurance written specifically to cover as excess over the limits of liability that apply in this policy.

SECTION I AND SECTION II - CONDITIONS

1. **Policy Period.** This policy applies only to loss under Section I or bodily injury or property damage under Section II which occurs during the period this policy is in effect.
2. **Concealment or Fraud.** This policy is void to you and any other insured, if you or any other insured under this policy has intentionally concealed or misrepresented any material fact or circumstance relating to this insurance, whether before or after a loss.
3. **Liberalization Clause**. If we adopt any revision which would broaden coverage under this policy without additional premium, within 60 days prior to or during the period this policy is in effect, the broadened coverage will immediately apply to this policy.
4. **Waiver or Change of Policy Provisions.** A waiver or change of any provision of this policy must be in writing by us to be valid. Our request for an appraisal or examination shall not waive any of our rights.
5. **Cancellation.**
   a. You may cancel this policy at any time by notifying us in writing of the date cancellation is to take effect. We may waive the requirement that the notice be in writing by confirming the date and time of cancellation to you in writing.
   b. We may cancel this policy only for the reasons stated in this condition. We will notify you in writing of the date cancellation takes effect. This cancellation notice may be delivered to you, or mailed to you at your mailing address shown in the Declarations. Proof of mailing shall be sufficient proof of notice. Upon receipt of written request from you, we shall furnish the facts of which the cancellation is based:
      (1) When you have not paid the premium, we may cancel at any time by notifying you at least 10 days before the date cancellation takes effect. This condition applies whether the premium is payable to us or our agent under any finance or credit plan.
      (2) When this policy has been in effect for less than 60 days and is not a renewal with us, we may cancel for any reason. We may cancel by notifying you at least 10 days before the date cancellation takes effect.
      (3) When this policy has been in effect for 60 days or more or at any time if it is a renewal with us, we may cancel if there has been:
         (a) conviction of a crime having as one of its necessary elements an act increasing the hazard insured against;
         (b) discovery of fraud or material misrepresentation;
         (c) discovery of grossly negligent acts or omissions substantially increasing any of the hazards insured against; or
         (d) physical changes in the property insured which result in the property becoming uninsurable.

         We may cancel this policy by notifying you at least 45 days before the date cancellation takes effect.
      (4) When this policy is written for a period longer than one year, we may cancel for any reason at anniversary. We may cancel by notifying you at least 45 days before the date cancellation takes effect.
   c. When this policy is canceled, the premium for the period from the date of cancellation to the expiration date will be refunded. When you request cancellation, the return premium will be based on our rules for such cancellation. The return premium may be less than a full pro rata refund. When we cancel, the return premium will be pro rata.
   d. If, when we cancel this policy, the return premium is not refunded with the notice of cancellation, we will refund it within 25 days after the date cancellation takes effect. If, when you cancel this policy, the return premium is not refunded when this policy is returned to us, we will refund it within a reasonable time after the date cancellation takes effect.
6. **Nonrenewal.** We may elect not to renew this policy. If we elect not to renew, a written notice will be delivered to you, or mailed to you at your mailing address shown in the Declarations. The Notice will be mailed or delivered at least 45 days before the expiration date of this policy. Proof of mailing shall be sufficient proof of notice.

   If this policy is written for a period of less than one year, we agree not to refuse to renew except at the end of an annual period commencing with the original or renewal effective date.
7. **Assignment.** Assignment of this policy shall not be valid unless we give our written consent.
8. **Subrogation.** An insured may waive in writing before a loss all rights of recovery against any person. If not waived, we may require an assignment of rights of recovery for a loss to the extent that payment is made by us.

   If an assignment is sought, an insured shall:
   a. sign and deliver all related papers;
   b. cooperate with us in a reasonable manner; and
   c. do nothing after a loss to prejudice such rights.

   Subrogation does not apply under Section II to Medical Payments to Others or Damage to Property of Others.
9. **Death**. If any person named in the Declarations or the spouse, if a resident of the same household, dies:
   a. we insure the legal representative of the deceased. This condition applies only with respect to the premises and property of the deceased covered under this policy at the time of death;
   b. insured includes:
      (1) any member of your household who is an insured at the time of your death, but only while a residence of the residence premises; and
      (2) with respect to your property, the person having proper temporary custody of the property until appointment and qualification of a legal representative.
10. **Conformity to State Law.** When a policy provision is in conflict with the applicable law of the State in which this policy is issued, the law of the State will apply.

WORKERS' COMPENSATION (Residence Employees)

COVERAGES

We will pay, with respect to residence employees:
1. Under Coverage I, when due, all benefits required of any insured by the California Workers' Compensation Law; and
2. Under Coverage II, on behalf of an insured, all damages for which the insured is legally liable because of bodily injury sustained by a residence employee. The bodily injury must be caused by accident or disease and arise out of and in the course of employment by the insured while:
   a. in the United States of America, its territories or possessions, or Canada; or
   b. temporarily elsewhere if the residence employee is a citizen or resident of the United States or Canada.

   Coverage II does not apply to any suit brought in or judgment rendered by any court outside the United States of America, its territories and possessions, or Canada, or to any action on such judgment.

   These coverages apply only to bodily injury which occurs during the policy period. If the bodily injury is a disease, it must be caused or aggravated by the conditions of the residence employee's employment by the insured.

SPECIAL DEFINITION

Residence employee, as used in this coverage, means an employee of any insured whose duties are incidental to the ownership, maintenance or use of the residence premises, including the performance of household domestic services, or whose duties are personal and not in the course of the trade, business, profession or occupation of any insured.

Residence employee does not include any person of whom the insured is the parent, spouse or child. Also, residence employee does not include any person who, during the 90 calendar days immediately preceding injury:
1. was employed by the insured for less than 52 hours; or
2. earned less than $100 in wages from an insured.

EXCLUSIONS

This coverage does not apply:
1. to liability for additional compensation imposed on an insured under Section 4553 and 4557, Division IV, Labor Code of the State of California, because of:
   a. the serious and willful misconduct of an insured; or
   b. bodily injury to an employee under 16 years of age and illegally employed at the time of injury;
2. to liability for bodily injury arising out of business pursuits of an insured;
3. to liability arising out of the discharge, harassment or coercion of, or the discrimination against any employee in violation of any law;
4. under Coverage II:
   a. to liability assumed by the insured under any contract or agreement;
   b. to bodily injury by disease unless a written claim is made or suit brought against the insured within 36 months after the end of the policy period;
   c. to any obligation under a workers' compensation, unemployment or disability benefits law or any similar law;
   d. to punitive or exemplary damages where insurance of liability therefor is prohibited by law or contrary to public policy;
   e. to bodily injury intentionally caused or aggravated by you.

LIMIT OF LIABILITY COVERAGE II

Our total limit of liability will not exceed $100,000 for all damages because of bodily injury:
1. sustained by one or more residence employees in any one accident; or
2. caused by disease and sustained by a residence employee.

Our total limit of liability will not exceed $500,000 for all damages arising out of bodily injury by disease regardless of the number of residence employees who sustain bodily injury by disease.

APPLICABLE POLICY PROVISIONS

The following policy provisions apply to this coverage:
1. The definitions of "you", "your", "we", "us", "our", "bodily injury", "business", "insured" and "residence premises";
2. Our agreement to defend the insured as provided under Coverage L - Personal Liability;
3. **Section II - Additional Coverages, items:**

SAMPLE OF A REPLACEMENT COST POLICY

NOTE: THIS REPRODUCTION DOES NOT NECESSARILY REFLECT THE COVERAGES ON YOUR OWN HOMEOWNER POLICY.

PAGE 6

1. Claim Expenses; and
2. First Aid Expenses;

4\. **Section II - Conditions, items:**

3\. Duties After Loss; and
6\. Suit Against Us;

5\. **Section I and Section II - Conditions, items:**

4\. Waiver or Change of Policy Provisions;
5\. Cancellation;
7\. Assignment; and
8\. Subrogation.

ADDITIONAL POLICY PROVISIONS

The following additional provisions apply:

1. Under Coverage I:
   a. We will be directly and primarily liable to any residence employee of any insured entitled to the benefits of the California Workers' Compensation Law;
   b. As between the residence employee and us, notice to or knowledge of the occurrence of the injury on the part of an insured will be deemed notice or knowledge on our part;
   c. The jurisdiction of any insured will, for the purpose of the law imposing liability for compensation, be our jurisdiction;
   d. We will be subject to the orders, findings, decisions or awards rendered against an insured, under the provisions of the law imposing liability for compensation, subject to the provisions, conditions and limitations of this policy. This policy shall govern as between an insured and us as to payments by either in discharge of an insured's liability for compensation;
   e. The residence employee has a first lien upon any amount which we owe you on account of this insurance. In case of your legal incapacity or inability to receive the money and pay it to the residence employee, we will pay it directly to the residence employee. Your obligation to the residence employee will be discharged to the extent of such payment; and
   f. The law mandates that you reimburse us for penalties we are required to pay the injured employee. We are required to pay a 10% penalty of the late payment if the late payment which gives rise to an increased payment is due less than 7 days after we receive the completed claim form from the employer.

   We will notify you in writing, within 30 days of the payment and will bill and collect the amount of the penalty. You are not obligated to repay us unless the aggregate total paid in a policy year exceeds $100.

   You will have 60 days, following notice of the obligation to reimburse, to appeal the decision to the Department of Insurance.
2. Under Coverage I and Coverage II:
   a. Other Insurance. This coverage does not apply to any loss to which other valid and collectible Workers' Compensation or Employers' Liability Insurance applies.
   b. Conformity to Statute. Terms of this coverage which are in conflict with the California Workers' Compensation Law are amended to conform to that law.

OPTIONAL POLICY PROVISIONS

The following Optional Policy Provisions are subject to all the terms and provisions of this policy, unless otherwise indicated in the terms of the option.

Each Optional Policy Provision applies only as indicated in the Declarations.

Option AI - Additional Insured. The definition of insured is extended to include the person or organization named in the Declarations as an Additional Insured or whose name is one file with us. Coverage is with respect to:

1. Section 1 - Coverage A; or
2. Section II - Coverages L and M but only with respect to the residence premises. This coverage does not apply to bodily injury to an employee arising out of or in the course of the employee's employment by the person or organization.

This option applies only with respect to the location show in the Declarations.

Option BP - Business Property.

COVERAGE B - PERSONAL PROPERTY, Special Limits of Liability, item b. is changed as follows:

The $1,000 limit is replace with the amount shown in the Declarations for this option.

Option BU - Business Pursuits.

Section II - Exclusion 1.b. is modified as follows:

1. Section II coverage applies to the business pursuits of an insured who is a:
   a. clerical office employee, salesperson, collector, messenger; or
   b. teacher (except college, university and professional athletic coaches), school principal or school administrator;

   while acting within the scope of the above listed occupations.
2. However, no coverage is provided:
   a. for bodily injury or property damage arising out of a business owned or financially controlled by the insured or by a partnership of which the insured is a partner or member;
   b. for bodily injury or property damage arising out of the rendering of or failure to render professional services of any nature (other than teaching or school administration). This exclusion includes but is not limit to:
      (1) architectural, engineering or industrial design services;
      (2) medical, surgical, dental or other services or treatment conducive to the health of persons or animals; and
      (3) beauty or barber services or treatment;
   c. for bodily injury to a fellow employee of the insured injured in the course of employment; or
   d. when the insured is a member of the faculty or teach staff of a school or college:
      (1) for bodily injury or property damage arising out of the maintenance, use, loading or unloading of:
         (a) draft or saddle animals, including vehicles for use with them; or
         (b) aircraft, motor vehicles, recreational motor vehicles or watercraft, airboats, air cushions or personal watercraft which use a water jet pump powered by an internal combustion engine as the primary source of propulsion;

         owned or operated, or hired by or for the insured or employer of the insured or used by the insured for the purpose of instruction in the use thereof; or
      (2) under Coverage M for bodily injury to a pupil arising out of corporal punishment administered by or at the direction of the insured.

Option FA - Firearms. Firearms are insured for accidental direct physical loss or damage.

The limits for this option are shown in the Declarations. The first amount is the limit for any one article; the second amount is the aggregate limit for each loss.

The following additional provisions apply:

1. we do not insure for any loss to the property described in this option either consisting of, or directly and immediately caused by, one or more of the following:
   a. mechanical breakdown, wear and tear, gradual deterioration;
   b. insects or vermin;
   c. any process of refinishing, renovating, or repairing;
   d. dampness of atmosphere or extremes of temperatures;
   e. inherent defect or faulty manufacture;
   f. rust, fouling or explosion of firearms;
   g. breakage, marring, scratching, tearing or denting unless caused by fire, thieves or accidents to conveyances; or
   h. infidelity of an insured's employees or persons to whom the insured property may be entrusted or rented;
2. our limit for loss by any Coverage B peril except theft is the limit shown in the Declarations for Coverage B, plus the aggregate limit;
3. our limits for loss by theft are those shown in the Declarations for this option. These limits apply in lieu of the Coverage B theft limit; and
4. our limits for loss by any covered peril except those in items 2. and 3. are those shown in the Declarations.

Option HC - Home Computer. The Section I - Special Limits for Liability for electronic data processing equipment and the recording or storage media used with that equipment is increased to be the amount shown on the Declarations for this option.

Option IO - Incidental Business. The coverage provided by this option applies only to that incidental business occupancy on file with us.

1. Section I: COVERAGE B - PERSONAL PROPERTY is extended to include equipment, supplies and furnishings usual and incidental to this business occupancy. This Option Policy Provision does not include electronic data processing equipment or the recording or storage media used with that equipment or merchandise held as samples or for sale or for delivery after sale.

   The Option IO limits are shown in the Declarations. The first limit applies to property on the residence premises. The second limit applies to property while off the residence premises. These limits are in addition to the Section I, COVERAGE B- PERSONAL PROPERTY, Special Limits of Liability on property used or intended for use in a business.
2. Section II: The residence premises is not considered business property because an insured occupies a part of it as an incidental business.
3. Section II: Exclusion 1.b. of Coverage L and Coverage M is replaced with the following:
   b. bodily injury or property damage arising out of business pursuits of an insured or the rental or holding for rental of any part of any premises by an insured. This exclusion does not apply:
      (1) to activities which are ordinarily incidental to non-business pursuits or to business pursuits of any insured which are necessary or incidental to the use of the residence premises as an incidental business;
      (2) with respect to Coverage L to the occasional or part-time business pursuits of an insured who is under 19 years of age;
      (3) to the rental or holding for rental of a residence of yours:
         (a) on an occasional basis for exclusive use as a residence;
         (b) in part, unless intended for use as a residence by more than two roomers or boarders; or
         (c) in part, as in incidental business or private garage;
      (4) when the dwelling on the residence premises is a two family dwelling and you occupy one part and rent or hold for rental the other part; or
      (5) to farm land (without buildings) not in excess of 500 acres, rented or held for rental to others.
4. This insurance does not apply to:
   a. bodily injury to an employee of an insured arising out of the residence premises as an incidental business other than to a residence employee while engaged in the employee's employment by an insured;
   b. bodily injury to a pupil arising out of corporal punishment administered by or at the direction of the insured;
   c. liability arising out of any acts, errors or omissions of an insured, or any other person for whose acts an insured is liable, resulting from the preparation or approval of data, plans, designs, opinions, reports, programs, specifications, supervisory inspections or engineering services in the conduct of an insured's incidental business involving data processing, computer consulting or computer programming; or
   d. any claim made or suit brought against any insured by:
      (1) any person who is in the care of any insured because of child care services provided by or at the direction of:
         (a) any insured;
         (b) any employee of any insured; or
         (c) any other person actually or apparently acting on behalf of any insured; or
      (2) any person who makes a claim because of bodily injury to any person who is in the care of any insured because of child care services provided or at the direction of:
         (a) any insured;
         (b) any employee of any insured; or
         (c) any other person actually or apparently acting on behalf of any insured.

      Coverage M does not apply to any person indicated in (1) or (2) above.

      This exclusion does not apply to the occasional child care services provided by any insured, or to the part-time child care services provided by any insured who is under 19 years of age.

Option JF - Jewelry and Furs. Under SECTION I - ADDITIONAL COVERAGES, item 10. is changed as follows:

1. the "$1,500" limit is replaced with the first amount shown in the Declarations for this option; and
2. the "$2,500" limit is replaced with the second amount shown in the Declarations for this option.

Option SG - Silverware and Goldware Theft. The theft limit on silverware and goldware is increased to be the amount shown in the Declarations for this option.

IN WITNESS WHEREOF, this Company has executed and attested these presents; but this policy shall not be valid unless countersigned by the duly authorized Agent of this Company at the agency hereinbefore mentioned.

____________________ Secretary

____________________ President

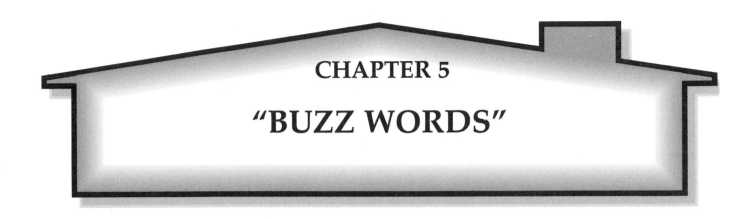

CHAPTER 5

"BUZZ WORDS"

• KNOW THE INSURANCE BUZZ WORDS

INSURANCE BUZZ WORDS

It is important to understand certain insurance terms when you evaluate your policy and/or attempt to settle your claim for damages.

As a policyholder negotiating the settlement of an insurance claim, you are involved in a business negotiation. It may be hard to be objective, as you will have a personal and emotional view of your situation. To the insurance company, its representatives and courts that may eventually become involved in your claim, the situation is strictly business, and contract conditions and legal precedents will not be modified to comply with your personal sentiments.

Claims submissions, negotiation and settlement terminology from one insurance company to the other can vary, but the following common terms may assist you in understanding what your insurance company is talking about.

Actual Cash Value (ACV)

A dollar value placed on damaged property equal to replacement cost less depreciation. Actual cash value is derived by fixing a new price for the same or similar item and deducting for wear and tear and obsolescence.

Additional Living Expenses

Any additional expenses incurred for food, lodging, transportation, and other daily needs, resulting from an insured loss.

Adjuster

One who represents the insurer or homeowner in arranging settlement of a claim. See claims representative, independent adjusters, public adjuster.

Agent

One who solicits insurance business on behalf of the insurer. An employee of the insurance company for the sale and service of insurance contracts.

All Risk Policy

"All risk" coverage means it protects against loss by any cause, <u>except</u> those items specifically excluded.

Appraisal

A valuation of property by disinterested persons of suitable qualifications.

Appurtenant Structures

Something belonging or incidental to a principal structure. An appurtenant structure to a home may be a garage, barn, playhouse, storage shed, etc. Structures on the property that are not attached to the home.

Arbitration

A method of resolving disputes through the assistance of an impartial (third) party. The parties to the dispute agree on the arbitrator to be used and to abide by the arbitrator's decision. Insurance arbitration is binding on both parties.

Assignment of Claim

An assignment of claim is a document that you sign in order for the restoration contractor to represent you to the insurance company on your behalf.

The advantage of assigning your claim to a qualified restoration contractor is that the contractor can handle your insurance claim and the repair work from start to finish, for usually just the amount of your deductible.

You may also be asked to sign, along with the assignment of claim, a special power of attorney. This document should be limited to authorizing your restoration contractor to represent you only for the specific claim, and should be deemed void upon completion of the work and final claim settlement.

Bad Faith

This generally means not dealing fairly. If your insurance company denies your claim without a valid reason, they may be dealing in "bad faith." If their settlement offer is unreasonably low, and they refuse to discuss settlement anymore, they may be in bad faith. An act of willful deception in furtherance of a sinister or dishonest motive.

Betterment

An improvement to property which increases its value. The improvement is characterized by increasing the value more than would mere replacement, repair or maintenance.

Bid

Promise to perform work for a certain price. An offer to provide services which become legally binding upon acceptance.

Board up (Coverup)

Emergency repairs to secure property from further damages or loss.

Broker

One who solicits insurance on behalf of several insurers. See Agent.

Building Code Upgrade Coverage

Building code upgrade coverage requires an "endorsement" or addition to your existing policy coverage. This coverage is designed to afford protection to you for the everchanging safety and environmental legislative and regulatory modifications. It will cost an additional fee to have this kind of coverage attached to your existing policy. For example, this kind of coverage can affect electrical, plumbing and structural code changes. Code changes could prove to be extremely costly if not protected by this kind of policy endorsement.

Building Equipment

Includes propane and oil tanks, storm windows, tools used to maintain the property, and similar items.

Catastrophe Unit

When a major disaster strikes, such as a hurricane, tornado, earthquake, etc., insurers send a large contingency of adjusters to evaluate claims in the damaged area. A "CAT unit," as they are commonly called, is an immediate, emergency-focused unit comprising of insurance representatives of all types. These adjusters may not have the expertise to evaluate certain claims since they are dispatched in emergency situations quickly and may not be working within their usual sphere of knowledge. Their main function is to provide assistance to the homeowner in submitting claims in an expeditious manner, and to "be on the scene" to pay temporary expenses or to provide other insurance-covered immediate needs.

Claim

Notification of loss and extent of damages suffered. Includes information relating to coverage, type of peril, what was lost, value of loss, and evidence of loss.

Claimant

The person who has legal standing to file a claim.

Claim Number

The claim number is assigned to your claim when notification is made to the insurance company. This number is used to track your contact, communications and file progress.

Claims Representative

Employee of insurance company, who negotiates settlement on behalf of his employer.

Concealment

The intentional withholding of information that one has a duty to reveal. Such information being necessary for the determination of coverage but withheld for purposes of benefiting either; from something not entitled to under the policy, or something entitled to in the policy but not known to the insured.

Condition

A provision in an insurance policy which sets out the rights and duties of the parties involved, or describes the events under which protection is granted.

Contents

Unscheduled personal property is usually described as the "contents." It is called "unscheduled" because the contents are grouped within a broad category with-out listing specific items. It includes furniture, clothing, books, appliances, and other personal property.

Coverage

The amount and extent of protection under an insurance contract.

Damages

The dollar amount awarded to an injured party for losses suffered at the hands of anothers unlawful acts, omissions or negligence. Damages are for compensating an injured party for their loss (Compensatory) and in some cases for punishing the wrongdoer (Punitive).

Deductible

The deductible is paid directly by the homeowner and is the amount that must be exceeded in damage costs before your insurance company becomes liable under a covered claim.

Depreciation

A reduction of worth arising from age, use or obsolescence. Depreciation is usually determined by calculating the difference between how long an item is in use against its life expectancy. Insurance companies have guidelines which can be used for this purpose, however, it is important to understand that there is considerable variation in determining the life expectancy of an item and the guidelines should be adjusted accordingly.

The following is an approximation chart of certain parts of your home's structure and examples of common depreciation rates per year. This list has been compiled from various contractors and insurance sources.

PART OF STRUCTURE	RATE OF DEPRECIATION
Shake roof	4 - 5 %
Composition roofs	5 %
Exterior paint	15 - 20 %
Interior paint	10 - 20 %
Vinyl sheet flooring	5 - 10 %
Floor tile	4 - 7 %
Hardwood floor finish	4 - 10 %

Carpet	10 - 20	%
Electrical wiring	4	%
Water heaters	4 - 7	%
Heaters and air conditioning	3 - 5	%

Once you have agreed with the insurance adjuster on the amount of a settlement, you may be surprised when it arrives, that approximately 10 percent of the dwelling settlement has been withheld for depreciation. That is done to protect the insurance company should you decide not to replace everything contained in the claim.

If you decide on a contractor to rebuild or replace your loss, the insurance company will normally withhold this amount (10%) until the work is completed. You must then make a request within the time requirements of your own policy for the withheld depreciation amount to be returned by the insurance company.

If your policy is issued with full provisions of "Replacement Cost Coverage," your final settlement can be determined by your insurance company in three different ways. Please see "Replacement Cost" in this section.

Dwelling

This is the structure described in the policy as the primary residence covered by the insurance policy.

Endorsements

An endorsement is a document provided by your insurance carrier that may provide additional coverage for specific items not covered by the original policy. The basic homeowners policy covers personal property in general, called "unscheduled" personal property. Personal property covered under an endorsement policy is specifically "scheduled" meaning the property is listed and described separately, and should be covered in a loss.

Estimate

A rough approximation of restoration costs having no promise to perform.

Exclusion

Provisions in the policy which state certain circumstances that bar coverage.

Fiduciary

Business relations between parties, in which one party has practically full control over terms of contract, and is thereby held to the highest degree of trust, confidence, fairness and good faith to the other.

Fixtures

Fixtures are personal property that are considered real property when permanently attached to the building, and may include items such as blinds, shades, mirrors, built-in shelves, awnings, lighting and other such property.

Floater

Policy endorsement, which covers items that have no fixed location such as jewelry or personal property while traveling. The terms floater policy and floating policy are often used in place of endorsement.

Fraud

A deceptive representation, whether by word, conduct, concealment or implication, which another relies on to his detriment. See Bad faith.

General Conditions

The "General Conditions" section of your policy outlines several policy provisions and requirements and also contains various conditions and exclusions.

Guaranty

A pledge or promise that materials and workmanship meet accepted standards, and in the event of a discovered defect or default, the promise will replace or repair.

Homeowners Policy

A multi-peril insurance policy covering such hazards as fire, water, burglary, liability, etc.

Hidden Damage

Damages which are not discoverable under reasonable inspection.

Indemnify

To make good, to restore a victim of a loss, by payment, repair or replacement.

Independent Adjuster

A person or firm who holds himself or itself out for the employment of claims adjustment to more than one insurance company.

Insurance Commissioner

Each state has an Insurance Commissioner. Most are appointed by the Governor of the state, although some are elected officials. The Insurance Commissioner's office is given the task of monitoring the activities of insurance companies, assuring proper compliance with state laws regulating insurance companies and monitoring whether companies are solvent (able to meet all financial responsibilities).

Insured

The buyer of an insurance policy, the homeowner.

Insured Loss

Damages or loss covered by homeowner's policy.

Insurer

The insurance company or underwriter.

Investigation

This is the procedure an insurance representative (adjuster) is obligated to follow in order to create the claim file for the insurance company. Don't be intimidated by the term "investigation." The company is not investigating you (unless you have a history of fraudulent claims), it is merely investigating to determine their responsibilities in paying your claim.

Liability Insurance

Insurance protection that covers injuries to others.

Lien Release

A waiver of lien rights, signed by subcontractors, so that the general contractor can receive a progress payment for work completed.

Limits

The maximum amount an insurance company will pay on a particular loss.

Line Item Bid

A detailed bid for restoration work listing each area of restoration and its cost.

Living Expenses

If the dwelling becomes uninhabitable because of a loss covered in the policy, the insurance company should pay the costs of living over and above what the insured normally spends.

Loss

Injury or damage sustained by policyholder which is the basis for filing a claim.

Loss of Use

Additional expenses incurred as a result of the homeowner's loss of property. See Additional Living Expenses.

Loss Payable Clause

Provision in homeowner's policy which authorizes payment to others (mortgage company, deed of trust, etc.) having legal interest in the property.

Low Ball

Term used within the insurance industry that indicates an estimate that is too low to be considered a reasonable estimate for completing repairs properly.

Mediation

A voluntary, legally non-binding, method of resolving a dispute with the assistance of a neutral party.

Mediator

One who intermediates between disputants to affect a mutual understanding and agreement.

Medical Payments

If a person is injured on your property, medical expenses are generally covered up to your policy limits. In addition, most off-the-premises injuries are also covered. For example, if your golf ball strikes and injures another golfer, the insurer should pay for the injury.

Mitigate

To reduce the potential of further damage or lessen the degree of what has already been damaged.

Mortgage Inspector

A representative of a mortgage holder who verifies work progress of restorations to an insured dwelling, in order to release some or all funds for payment.

Negligence

Failure to use a reasonable amount of care. Falling below that standard of care used by a reasonably prudent and careful person under similar circumstances.

Outdoor Equipment

May include lawn mowers, small tractors, outdoor furniture, gas barbecues, etc.

Payee

An individual or business named on a settlement draft or check.

Peril

A peril is a natural event (wind, rain, snow, etc.) which may cause damage covered by an insurance carrier, provided you have purchased the necessary protection through valid coverage.

Personal Liability

You are insured for up to your policy limits if you or a member of your family accidentally injures someone or damages someone's property and he/she, in turn, sues you. You should be protected both on and off the premises for a wide variety of mishaps. For example, you are protected if someone injures his or herself by falling down your front stairs, or by slipping on your sidewalk, or even if your dog runs down the street and bites the mailman.

Policy Limits

Virtually all property coverage policies indicate a policy limit. The terminology used for "policy limit" can be those very words or can be expressed as "amount of insurance," "limit of insurance," or "limit of liability." Policy limits are normally the maximum that can be paid on the claim regardless of the actual value of the property damaged.

Premium

The amount of money a homeowner pays for insurance, the cost of coverage.

Proof of Loss

A claimant's formal statement to the insurer which is used to determine the insurer's extent of liability.

Proof of Loss Form

This is a form provided by either your agent or your claims office. It is required to be submitted with your claim for damages. It is a document which asks you, the policyholder, to provide information concerning your loss. There is space provided for a brief description of your loss, but you should not rely on this minimal information site to settle your claim. You must attach separate paperwork which substantiates your expenses, estimates of repair, and settlement request. Be aware that in the event of a lawsuit, any information in writing may be obtained in a court of law as evidence. Be as accurate as possible!

Proximate Cause

The initial damage, which caused further damage by an unbroken chain of events, is referred to as the proximate cause.

Public Adjusters

A public adjuster is a person who, for compensation, acts on behalf of or aids an insured in the settlement of a claim for loss or damage under an insurance policy covering real or personal property.

Release

The document usually required by the insurer to be executed by the claimant before payment of a claim is made. Be aware that the general rule in signing a release is that the claimant waives any right to further action against the insurer. Some settlement drafts contain language on the endorsee side that, in effect, is a waiver of the claimant's rights to pursue related litigation against the insurer such as bad faith actions and misrepresentations. Be sure to carefully look for any "release language" on checks or letters the insurance company may issue to you and/or consult with an attorney if necessary.

Replacement Cost

Replacement cost generally means that the insurance carrier is responsible for the full cost of repair or replacement of the damaged property, without deducting for improvements or depreciation.

When claims are paid under the replacement cost coverage in the homeowners policy, the insurance carrier can figure its obligation three different ways and choose the one that works best financially for the them:

1) Based on the policy limits—the most the company ever will pay is the amount of insurance that applies to the property covered, be it a dwelling or an appurtenant structure.

2) Based on the cost of replacement—based on the cost of an equivalent building in the vicinity.

3) Based on the actual amount spent in completing repairs.

In the case of losses over $1,000, the policyholder usually must complete repairs in order to collect the full amount of replacement costs. For its part, the insurance company is required to pay the amount of the actual cash value of the repairs. The difference between the actual cash value amount and the full replacement cost is paid after the policyholder shows that the work has been done and substantiates the cost of the work. Before a homeowner does any code upgrades, he/she should check their policy to see if upgrades are covered.

The policyholder also has another obligation in the matter of replacement cost claims for recovering withheld depreciation. He/she must take some form of action on a replacement cost claim usually within 180 days from the date of loss. Check your own policy for time limits regarding withheld depreciation because clauses vary from carrier to carrier.

Reserves

Reserves are estimates the insurance company makes through their claims evaluation that are set aside in order to pay anticipated claims. By placing estimate amounts in "reserve," the insurance company is free to invest this money while awaiting your final settlement.

Restoration Contractors

The most versatile of all types of contractors, the qualified restoration contractor is not only experienced in damage evaluation, scope of repairs, and claims processing, but in the actual restoration of your home and property.

Resultant Damage

Damage which has been caused as a direct result of an unbroken chain of events from a proximate cause.

Rider

An addition or amendment to a policy which is attached to and incorporated into the terms of the policy. See endorsement.

Scope of Damages

A contractor's list of structural damages, combined with an explanation of the method of repair and their cost.

Scope of Repair

An organized and concise written detailed estimate of the necessary repairs and actions that must take place in order to bring about a complete restoration of your home.

Settlement Demand

The settlement demand is normally the amount of money that you are requesting your insurance company to pay for the repair or replacement of your damage or loss. In property claims, this amount is based either on your cost to repair or on the estimate provided by your contractor.

Statements

There are two kinds of statements you may or may not be asked by your insurance company to participate in. The first is the informal statement, usually handwritten or recorded, to ascertain the facts surrounding a loss. The other kind of statement is a formal statement under oath. These statements normally pertain to theft claims and are usually not required in a property claim.

Subrogation

The transference of legal rights from the homeowner to the insurance company in order to recover from a third party. For example, an insurance company pays you on a claim and then sues a third party to recover the claim amount. The claim you have against the third party is transferred, or subrogated, to the insurer.

Subsidence

The sinking, upheaval or movement of land and the damages attributed to such. For example, cracks in foundation caused by settling is a form of subsidence.

Sudden and Accidental

An unexpected, unforeseen casualty or loss, as opposed to something that results from a continuous action. A requirement for recovery in a homeowner's claim.

Supplemental

An addition to the original claim for newly discovered hidden damages.

Telephone Log

This is a record of all communications that you have with your insurance company. The insurance company representative has been trained to maintain a log within the claim file. In case the representative leaves his employment, becomes sick or is replaced, another representative can take over where the previous representative left off. You should create and maintain your own settlement file and include a telephone/communications log of your own. Simply enter the date when you make contact with the insurance company and/or agent, and summarize the conversation or request of the insurance company for additional information or documentation. Get names of the people you speak with and write down anything that the representative might say which is contrary to your settlement position. If you call and the party you want to speak with is out, note that as well.

Umbrella Policy

An umbrella policy acts as a supplemental liability insurance policy, which can supplement not only your homeowners policy, but also other policies providing liability coverage. The umbrella policy is only excess insurance and usually does not come into play until the limits of the standard policy are exhausted.

Valuation

Valuation is the act or process of determining the amount that the policy will pay on insured property which is damaged by a covered peril.

Umpire

A third person appointed to decide an arbitration.

Zoning Ordinance

Exercise of police power of a municipality in regulating and controlling the character and use of property.

CHAPTER 6
SUBSTANTIATING & VALIDATING YOUR CLAIM

- **ELEMENTS OF A VALID LOSS**

- **SUBSTANTIATION AND VALIDATION**

- **PHOTOGRAPHS AND VIDEO**

- **BE ETHICAL**

- **RESTORATION CONTRACTOR ASSISTANCE**

- **MEETING YOUR ADJUSTER**

ELEMENTS OF A VALID LOSS

The following four criteria should be met in order for a loss to be covered by insurance:

- Losses must be accidental

    Accidental losses are opposed to events that are certain to occur. A loss caused by an event that is certain to occur would not constitute a valid insurance claim. The reason for the stipulation that losses must be accidental is that insurance policies insure against "risks." If a loss is certain to occur, there is no risk involved. An example is the proverbial baseball through the window. This "accident" is not certain to occur, but there is a chance that it may.

- Losses must be caused by an extraneous factor

    This means the loss must be caused by an external act or object. The loss cannot be caused by an inherent physical condition (wear and tear). An example of this covered loss is wind damage to your roof.

- Losses must not be caused by deliberate actions

    Deliberate actions, on the part of the policyholder, are not covered.

    For example: If you intentionally punch the wall or break a window, the insurance company will most likely deny your claim.

Keep photo negatives in a safety deposit box to preserve photographic evidence in the event of a loss to your property.

• Losses must not involve illegal property

   Contraband or illegal items are not covered by insurance. For example: Your illegal whiskey still in your attached garage blows up and you submit a claim for damages. Every single insurance company should deny this claim.

   It should also be noted that in order to have a valid claim, you must actually sustain a loss. For example, if you are in the initial stages of tearing down a detached garage in order to build a new one, and a storm hits and destroys the remaining structure destined for demolition, your claim probably would be denied.

SUBSTANTIATION AND VALIDATION

Sufficient substantiation of your loss supported with historical evidence helps determine whether or not your insurance carrier will accept liability in paying for your claim. The first thing to establish is who is going to accept liability.

The second consideration is to get current validation for your claim. Your claim for damages must be accompanied by proof of your damages. Documentary evidence or expert opinion statements can support your claim of loss, and provide you and the insurance company a basis in which to negotiate the settlement of your claim.

ESTABLISHING LIABILITY

The first and most important factor in substantiating whether you have a valid claim or not is the question of who is going to pay for the damage or, in other words, who is liable. You have paid for insurance protection by purchasing your insurance policy. If the damage to your property is covered under your policy and the insurance company accepts liability, then the insurance company is responsible for the payment of that loss. After it is determined if the insurance carrier will accept liability, it is important to know as well if that acceptance will cover the entire loss or just part of it.

You have previously learned in this publication that proximate cause is the doctrine followed by the insurance industry to help determine liability. The doctrine of proximate cause means that if the initial cause of damage is covered under your insurance policy, the resultant damage should be covered as well. It becomes the responsibility of the insurance carrier to cover the loss through settlement payment, notwithstanding any intervening force or event that may increase the damage.

With that in mind, let us explore some of the things that will assist you in establishing proof of your loss.

HISTORY OF YOUR PROPERTY

Establishing the history of the home you own is somewhat overlooked. Be sure to find an old photo of your home to document the condition of the dwelling prior to your property damage loss. Establishing a historical "picture" can be a very simple task if you use some creative thinking. Ask yourself the following questions: Prior to your ownership were there any inspections done on the property? Are you aware of any construction, renovation, or modification to the property? Were there any building permits obtained prior to your occupancy? Were there any geological reports filed with the city, town or county where your home is located?

These are questions that could affect your insurance damage claim substantially. For example: You have recently bought a new home and have suffered a loss caused by a broken water pipe under the foundation. The obvious resultant damage may be buckling of the floor and some wall damage but now, a week later, you discover that the foundation of your home has suddenly shifted and your "castle" is slipping into the canyon below. You may encounter an insurance adjuster who will say, "We can't honor this claim because this damage was caused by earth movement and earth movement is excluded from our coverage." But you have discovered (in your historical data search of the property) that a geological survey had been done on your property six months before you purchased it and the survey substantiates your claim by indicating that your home was built on a bed of rock capable of withstanding anything nature could dole out. The results of the survey may cause the insurance company adjuster to reconsider his/her position in regard to the coverage on your claim.

Another valuable source of information concerning your house are your neighbors. Before you moved into the neighborhood, most of your immediate neighbors probably knew of problems the previous tenant had endured. Ask questions of your neighbors and you will be able to elicit very useful information which may help you in substantiating your claim.

Be an aggressive detective!

USING EXPERTS TO VALIDATE YOUR CLAIM

All insurance claims are unique in their causes and circumstances. Some claims call for a thorough evaluation conducted by experts familiar with losses such as the one your have suffered. Written reports and opinions from experts are a tremendous source of validation to your claim.

For example, if your property has sustained a structural loss such as a cracked foundation or slab and you are unsure as to the cause, you may need to bring in the experts to help determine the proximate cause. In many cases this would call for bringing in not only a soils engineer but also a structural engineer.

Many of us have a fear of using such "experts" because it sounds like the cost of these services may even exceed the original claim. However, take heart that most experts (roof, soils, structural, and foundational engineers, etc.) will be very accommodating with your inquiries, sometimes at minimal or no charge. You can arrange for one or more of these experts to visit your home, assess your damage and give you an overview of what the cost might be to restore your property. Taking the simple step of having an expert examine your damaged area helps prepare you for your meeting with the insurance adjuster. It gives you prior knowledge of the factors being considered in your claim, as well as exposure to the language used between expert and adjuster. It can also boost your confidence in negotiating the settlement of your claim.

One thing to keep in mind is that you do not want to ask the expert to put his/her opinion and recommendations in a report until you feel you need documentation to validate your claim. The cost for the report will come directly out of your pocket unless your policy specifically covers the cost of such items.

In all cases, make sure the expert(s) you bring in to validate your claim supports <u>your</u> position of the contributing and/or direct cause of your damage.

PHOTOGRAPHS AND VIDEO

Take photographs or videos of any damage to your house or other buildings on the property. You can never have enough photographs or video. This can assist you and your carrier in evaluating the damage.

It is also a good idea to take pictures of the exterior of your home, even though your loss may be in the interior of your house. This will document the neighborhood and surrounding areas that may be a deciding factor to establish the value of your home, and the components contained therein.

Old Photos

Family and friends are a great source for producing older photographs which prove the existence or condition of property prior to the loss. These photos can be used to establish that no pre-existing condition or damage existed. They can also serve to assist in pricing out items totally destroyed, such as in the case of fire.

BE ETHICAL

Nothing can be gained when submitting an insurance claim if you have succumbed to the temptation to over-inflate your claim, or to present a claim for damage that pre-existed prior to the loss. It is not only morally wrong, it is unlawful, and can result in criminal prosecution.

Most insurance company adjusters have been experienced in the field long enough to know if someone is trying to pull one over on them.

If you have a legitimate loss and have confirmed coverage and protection the insurance company is responsible for, then be truthful and reasonable in your claim submission.

Entire claims, for large amounts of settlement monies, have been denied (and upheld by the courts) due to an exaggerated amount on one or two items of a claim. Be honest - your insurance will work for you - and you will feel better for it.

RESTORATION CONTRACTOR ASSISTANCE

The restoration contractor can help you in the assessment of your claim, and in determining whether or not you have a valid claim.

Visual inspections and detailed walk-throughs with the restoration contractor can help locate and identify damage you may have overlooked.

Again, because of the restoration contractor's experience with insurance companies, he/she can help evaluate whether or not your claim should be submitted to your carrier.

MEETING YOUR ADJUSTER

Generally, the first time you speak with your assigned adjuster on the telephone, it should give you a good idea of how the claim process works. Adjusters can be empathic, overzealous, non-compassionate or uncaring to your situation. This generally is a personality trait of a particular individual and not necessarily representative of other insurance personnel.

When the adjuster comes out to view your property the first time, your primary concern and focus should be to have a preliminary discussion of what caused the damage (the proximate cause). By this approach, you are attempting to establish whether or not the insurance carrier is going to accept liability and responsibility for the loss. You may get a quick response from the adjuster such as, "It looks like that storm last night really tore a hole in your roof. Under your policy you are covered completely for this loss."

But, on the contrary, the adjuster may comment, "That storm last night blew pretty hard but not hard enough to cause this damage."

In this situation, if the attention and conversation starts to wander away from determining the cause of the damage, you need to bring the conversation back into focus since the adjuster is not going to agree to pay for your damages until he/she accepts liability. Your objective here is to have the adjuster tell you what his/her position is going to be on the loss. If you can, get the adjuster to put his/her decision in writing. Once you know what the adjuster's position is, you can then decide what your next step should be.

If the adjuster has agreed to accept the liability and the the loss sustained is covered under your policy provisions, then you can proceed to discuss the resultant damages.

At this point, the adjuster will probably take measurements of the damaged area and photographs to establish his/her claim file. The adjuster may even offer you a settlement right then and there if the claim is minimal and within the adjuster's payment authority.

It is very important to remember that before you discuss settlement with the adjuster, you have prepared a detailed inventory of the damage. (See Chapter 8) Initially, it is important to look past just taking measurements of the damaged areas. Look out for items that might also be affected during the course of performing the restorations. Be sure to let the adjuster know that you will be preparing your claim package and that you will forward it to him/her when it is completed.

As you conduct the walk-through inspection with the insurance adjuster, video tape the entire process. This way you will have a permanent record of what has been pointed out and any comments made by the adjuster. You may find the adjuster is intimidated by the fact that you are creating a video record of the inspection, but explain to him/her that you just want to be absolutely certain that all areas of damage are accounted for and included in your claim. Be sure to let the adjuster know in advance of your intent to videotape the walk-through.

CHAPTER 7
PREPARING AND SUBMITTING YOUR CLAIM

- **UTILIZING YOUR CLAIMS FILE**

- **WHAT TO REQUEST FROM THE CLAIMS OFFICE**

- **CLAIM PREPARATION**

- **SUBMITTING YOUR CLAIM**

- **CLAIMS SUBMISSION CHECKLIST**

- **DO-IT-YOURSELF OR ASSIGN YOUR CLAIM TO A RESTORATION CONTRACTOR**

UTILIZING YOUR CLAIMS FILE

By this time, your file should have many entries, including all telephone calls and correspondence records between you and your insurance company representative.

If you have received correspondence from the insurance company, you should have saved the envelopes in which letters or notices were sent to you. These envelopes will display postmarks that may contradict the assigned adjuster's comment to you that he/she mailed your inquiry response three weeks ago even though you received it only yesterday!

Make photocopies of all your cancelled checks that you used to pay any expenses. These copies of cancelled checks will be used to submit for reimbursement, along with your final claims package.

Your current telephone bill may indicate the frequency of calls made to your adjuster. If he/she denies

that you placed a call on a particular date, you will have documentary proof of the calls you made. Most insurance companies, however, maintain efficient communications records.

Maintaining your file is essential, but now is the time to utilize the contents of that file. Continue to maintain the file as if you were preparing to go to trial over your claim. You most likely will never have to go that far in the process of your claim, but being prepared is the best way to prevent having to litigate.

WHAT TO REQUEST FROM THE CLAIMS OFFICE

- Request a claim number if you haven't already received one. The claim number that will be assigned to your file helps to track correspondence and will monitor your claim all the way through to the settlement and payment of your claim. Always refer to the claim number in all your communications with the insurance company whether written or oral.

- Ask for the name of your assigned adjuster if you don't already know who he/she is. Sometimes it takes a day or two for the insurance administration personnel to assign an adjuster, but be persistent. Also, request the assigned adjuster's direct telephone number, fax number, mailing address and usual business hours.

CLAIM PREPARATION

- Conduct a visual inspection of the damaged area

    Look for components not readily visible during a cursory inspection. Trace the damage and any resultant damage to walls, ceilings, flooring, etc.

- Make temporary repairs

    If your home has been damaged in a storm or fire, use plastic or boards to cover up any holes in the roof or walls to prevent further weather-related damage. Most insurance companies will reimburse you for the cost of temporary repairs, so be sure to save any receipts for materials. Don't make permanent repairs before consulting with your agent or claims adjuster.

- Contact your insurer or agent

    When you report a loss, your insurer will either send you a "Proof of Loss" form to complete or arrange for an adjuster to visit your home.

- You should document everything

    Document your loss as thoroughly as possible. If you prepared a written or video inventory before the loss, this task will be easier.

- Make a list of everything

    List everything damaged, including a detailed description of each item, the date of purchase and what it would cost to replace the items (if you have replacement-cost coverage).

- Gather relevant receipts

    Producing bills, photographs, or serial numbers (from appliances and electronic equipment) will help establish the value of your losses. The adjuster may want to see all of the damaged items so avoid throwing anything out.

- Make a list of the damaged areas

    Make a list of all the damaged areas and everything you want to show the adjuster, from cracks in the wall to missing roof tiles.

- Submit your claim

    Although most insurance companies require loss information and documentation to be submitted within 60 days, you generally have up to a year in which to amend your claim if you find additional damage or losses.

- Read your policy

    If you know what coverage you have, you're more likely to receive all you're entitled to receive. If you have any questions about your policy, call your agent.

- Call in the experts (see Chapter 13)

    If you have sustained structural damage to your home, do not attempt to "guesstimate" the cost of replacement or rebuilding. Contact an expert in this field immediately. A qualified restoration contractor, who may already be on hand to effect temporary repairs, may be a tremendous source for obtaining structural experts since they work in conjunction with these kinds of firms on a regular basis. If you need to, get all experts' reports, opinions and estimates in writing!

- Keep careful records

    Make copies of all information you give your insurer in connection with your claim. Also, be sure to hold onto everything the insurer gives you. It's also a good idea to take notes of all meetings and conversations you have with your agent, insurer and/or claims adjuster.

There are forms in Chapter 16 for you to use and modify depending on the nature of your claim.

SUBMITTING YOUR CLAIM

- Mail, deliver, or fax the assigned adjuster COPIES of your documentary evidence. This will include your "Proof of Loss" form (see Chapter 16), photographs of the damaged area or items, repair estimates, receipts and any other items being submitted to your adjuster or insurance company.

- It is best to send your information to the adjuster by certified mail, return receipt requested. That way you will receive a receipt of delivery. If you transmit your claim information by fax, you take the chance of your documentation not being routed to the proper adjuster. It also provides the insurance company the opportunity to give other excuses for not receiving your information.

- In claim submission correspondence, always demand that you expect a response no later than 30 days following receipt of your information and estimate of damage. Be sure to indicate an expected date for the insurance company to respond.

Remember that under a majority of insurance policies, the Loss Payment section (Section II- Conditions) states your insurance company is obligated to pay your loss within 30 days of submitting your proof of loss form provided:

a. you reach an agreement with your insurance company; or

b. there is an entry of a final judgment; or

c. there is a filing of an appraisal award with your insurance company.

CLAIMS SUBMISSION CHECKLIST

To assist you in the submission of your claim, there is a "Claims Submission Checklist," as well as other forms, in Chapter 16.

DO-IT-YOURSELF or ASSIGN YOUR CLAIM TO A RESTORATION CONTRACTOR

The processes involved in preparing and submitting your claim can be done by you depending on your time and resources. If you don't have the time or the resources, you might consider a qualified restoration contractor who has the experience and can handle the entire restoration process for you from start to finish.

CHAPTER 8
PREPARING THE "SCOPE OF REPAIRS"

- **WHAT IS A "SCOPE OF REPAIRS?"**

- **ORGANIZING THE "SCOPE OF REPAIRS"**

- **THE IMPORTANCE OF "LINE ITEM"**

- **LINE OF SIGHT RULE**

- **PRICING AND COSTS**

- **RESTORATION CONTRACTOR'S ROLE**

- **MEASUREMENTS MADE EASY**

- **SAMPLE JOB - "SCOPE OF REPAIRS"**

WHAT IS A "SCOPE OF REPAIRS?"

One of the most critical areas of the claims settlement process is the preparation of the written scope of damage, also commonly referred to as the "scope of repairs." At some point in time, you and the insurance adjuster will have one or more meetings to describe, in detail, the damage to the structure or item.

Some companies substitute other terms for scope. Common synonyms are "survey," "specifications," or "field notes." Regardless of the name, the scope is the first, and most critical, step in preparing a repair estimate.

Elements of a proper "Scope of Repairs"

- Description of the damage
- Line item of repair and costs
- Total cost of repair

The "scope of repairs" is an organized and concise layout of the damage or loss that you have sustained. The scope of repairs represents, in writing, the necessary repairs and actions that must take place in order to bring about a complete restoration to your home.

Aspects of the Loss to be Included in Complete Scope of Repairs:

- Structural
- Exterior, including insulation
- Room by room, including architectural items, finishes, fixtures and building systems contained within each room
- Floor
- Walls
- Trim, doors and windows
- Ceilings
- Fixtures, appliances, built-ins and cabinets
- Building systems that cross room boundaries such as plumbing, electrical and/or heating and air conditioning
- General considerations such as debris removal, access and permits

Considerations that affect the cost

There are numerous overlooked factors that affect the cost of your repair project. Some things are so unpredictable, such as weather, and some are so obvious that they are forgotten the moment restoration begins. For example, the extra dumpster that was needed at curbside is going to create an additional expense, thanks to the city's permit requirements.

Remember, just when you think you have covered all aspects of the cost of your project, go back over the sequence of the project and dig up those things that you have overlooked.

Here is a list of some of those considerations:

- Your home is on a hill, with a narrow road, making access by heavy equipment virtually impossible.
- The city street narrows in front of your home, making it difficult to place a dumpster at curbside.
- Tree removal.
- You suddenly realize your 30-foot cathedral ceiling is going to necessitate scaffolding that you never thought about before.
- The painter must remove all of the furniture in your bedroom, not just under the ceiling stain in the corner that needs to be painted.

- The city or association does not appreciate your workers commencing work with the power saws at 7:00 A.M. or on weekends and fines you $100.
- You hired an inexperienced carpet layer who takes double the time and money than that of an experienced one.
- Hanging a hollow core passage door requires one carpenter. Hanging a custom made solid oak door requires a carpenter and helper.
- Delays in obtaining building permits, licenses, etc.

ORGANIZING THE "SCOPE OF REPAIRS"

Begin by organizing the scope of repairs room by room or by area of damage. You should prepare a brief statement of what occurred that caused the damage and the repairs that need to take place. This will not only assist you in preparing a complete and detailed scope of repairs, but it can also be a reference of the facts of your loss that can be used by you during your negotiations with the insurance company.

Prepare a preliminary scope of repairs (pencil draft) before your formal presentation to the insurance company.

Upon your request, each contractor that you contact for estimation of repair and cost should provide you with a line item description and cost for repairs to be performed.

Use the contractor's information to complete and compute your scope of repairs.

Itemize line by line each and every repair action, required city permits, and/or required building permits. Give the cost of each line item.

Breakdown these costs further by unit cost, unit of measurement cost, price per unit and total cost.

Total all costs of all areas of repair and subtract your deductible amount.

The difference between the total cost of repairs (restoration) and your deductible will be the amount of your claim.

If you decide you do not want to assume the complexities and liability inherit in functioning as the general contractor, you do have another alternative. You can hire a qualified restoration contractor.

Qualified restoration contractors are the most adept at preparing a thorough scope of repairs. Since they are working daily with other tradespeople, their source of specialty contractors is selective and immediate. They have the expertise in the proper methods of scheduling and materials procurement. Their interaction with the insurance companies on a routine basis gives them an advantage, unlike other types of contractors, in getting the maximum repair coverage and settlement.

In all cases, you should not agree to any final scope of repairs until you are satisfied that it accurately reflects the loss of, or damage to, your home.

THE IMPORTANCE OF THE "LINE ITEM"

A line itemized scope of repairs provides an in-depth description and an exact detailed listing of the work to be performed, the materials to be used, equipment rental required, and any actions necessary to facilitate the repairs and cleanup in order to bring the room or area of damage to a full restoration. Your line item will also specify the cost by unit for materials, labor, equipment rental, and anything else needed to complete the repair.

Let's take the following example of some of the components included in a line item for a pantry area which has sustained a loss.

- Trash bin rental for debris removal.
- Remove, box up and reset pantry contents.
- Remove and replace solid oak quarter round shoe. Price reflects material, labor and installation.
- Install moisture barrier hardwood. Price reflects material, labor and installation.
- Oak strip flooring 3/4 x 2 #1 grade. Price reflects material, labor and installation.
- Sand, seal and varnish new hardwood floor.
- Polyurethane finish 2-coats new hardwood floor. Price reflects material, labor and installation.
- Apply new finish to quarter round to match floor.
- Final cleanup of area.

The most important function of line itemizing the scope of repairs is that it allows for any changes, modifications, and additional work that may affect the cost of the claim, and be deemed necessary for the full restoration of the damaged area.

The line itemization also affords protection to the homeowner by allowing flexibility in the submission of the claim concerning newly discovered damage, material substitution, and work scheduling.

Line itemization protects the tradespeople and contractor by stating exactly the work to be done and materials to be used, eliminating material purchase overruns and job related disputes.

Line itemization also protects the insurance company because they know exactly what work shall be done and at what cost, eliminating surprise charges and coverage disagreements.

An example of the benefits of line itemization is after the scope of repairs is completed and submitted to the insurance company you discover, while removing the hardwood flooring, that the subflooring is also damaged. You can then add additional line items of work and costs to make the repairs to the subflooring. The homeowner is now satisfied with the change, the contractor or tradesperson knows precisely what additional materials will be needed, and the insurance company will be assured that the job will be done properly without the need for another claim to be filed in the future over the newly discovered damage.

The new line item would indicate changes of work and materials to reflect the repair of the newly discovered damage and be a supplemental entry to the original claim.

LINE OF SIGHT RULE

This is a rather obscure insurance regulation found in one form or another in most states. It is found under the Standards of Extended Coverage with Replacement Cost Coverage commonly known as the "line of sight" rule. You may or may not be aware of this regulation because it essentially benefits the insured rather than the insurer. Insurance adjusters that have your best interests in mind will explain the benefits of this rule and how it will affect your claim, while others with different agendas will remain silent on the issue.

In the state of California the rule reads, "When a loss requires replacement of items and the replaced do not match in quality, color or size, the insurer shall replace all items in the damaged area so as to conform to a reasonably uniform appearance." The reason this regulation has acquired the industry phrase, "line of sight" is because materials in the damaged area of your claim have to conform.

In other words, insurers should not be allowed to "fix" a water-stained carpet by cutting out a patchwork piece and nailing down another piece that fails to match or conform to the rest of the carpet. The rule demands that the entire carpet be replaced in conformity within a clear "line of sight." Nor can an insurer demand that you accept roofing materials that do not match since the rule applies both to interior and exterior losses.

This rule, or a variation of it, is especially effective when you possess an insurance policy with "Full Replacement Coverage." Full Replacement Coverage is just what the terms imply: The item of damage must be entirely replaced if the materials suggested by the insurer do not conform in quality, color and size. You are not obligated to automatically accept the materials or workmanship the insurer is offering.

Most insurance adjusters are individuals of high integrity who are willing to consider information or policy interpretation, recognize and honor regulations set up to monitor the industry even if it benefits the insured. You should bear in mind though that the insurance adjuster assigned to your claim may not bring a "line of sight" type rule to your attention, you may want to consider a diplomatic inquiry directed to the adjuster to determine if this rule applies to your claim. It may even result in maximizing your claim!

This type of insurance code is generally in effect in a majority of states. Contact your Department of Insurance to verify whether or not your state has adopted a similar code.

PRICING AND COSTS

The next step in the estimation process is to price out the scope into a final rebuild or repair estimate. Any construction project involves the following type of costs:

- Materials
- Labor
- Tools and special equipment
- Overhead and profit (if applicable)
- Miscellaneous costs such as permits and taxes

If you are acting as the owner-builder/general contractor, the subcontractors you plan on using should also be a part of this estimation process. They will have information on the local prices of materials, can estimate labor costs, advise you of any tools and special equipment needed to adequately complete the job, and can determine the overhead and profit and the miscellaneous costs for the job.

Generally, there are two methods to determine costs. One method, commonly known as the "lump sum" method, is a method of developing a fixed dollar amount for the job to be performed by determining the total sum of all labor and materials costs. This method of pricing is extremely inadequate.

Because itemization of key components cannot be isolated, the quality of work may be overlooked in favor of completing the job within the limits of the total sum estimated for the job.

Any time a fixed amount is determined for the completion of a rebuild or repair of your property, many problems and questions can arise. Has the subcontractor assessed all the necessary rebuild and damage restoration? If the subcontractor discovers internal damage to structure or walls, will they ignore the damage to stay within the agreed upon "lump sum" price for job performance? If you are limited to the "bottom line" of the lump sum cost method, how will you submit any type of supplemental claim, should the need arise?

- An example of a problem that could arise when using the lump sum method would be if you received a quote from a subcontractor indicating that he/she would repair drywall for $200.00, including all materials and labor, only to find out after repairs have begun that more repair to the drywall is needed than originally thought.

The second, and most effective and accurate method to determine costs, is the unit cost estimate method.

The unit cost method relies on a detailed, itemized, and segregated listing of all labor costs for each item to be repaired. For example, the unit cost for painting a bedroom is established and a separate unit cost is determined to replace drywall damage in a ceiling quadrant. The painting, drywall, wallpaper, and spraying of acoustic ceilings should be determined by square feet. Carpet, stucco, and plaster should be determined by square yard. If additional damage, which exceeds the original footage, is discovered, then this method allows for the additional adjustments in the form of a supplemental claim.

- An example of the unit cost estimate method would be getting a quote to repair the same drywall, but pricing it out by line item.

(note: prices include labor and materials)

mask off to isolate work area   1 hr @ $27.00 = $ 27.00

remove damaged drywall 100 sq ft @ $ .35 = $ 35.00

install drywall   100 sq ft @ $1.38 = $138.00

Total for removal and installing drywall = $200.00

Whichever method is used, other considerations must be addressed in determining the cost of your project. Other considerations include, but are not limited to, demolition, debris removal, and the cost impact of the job. Following is a brief synopsis of each category:

a) Demolition is the removal of damaged components from their original place in the structure. The demolition labor figures include the time needed to pile the debris on the premises. As with any other operation, the adjuster can estimate this cost on either a "lump sum" method (labor and materials) or unit cost method.

b) Debris removal cost is the labor and expense involved in removing debris from the site. There are two general types of debris. The first is the debris of the damaged property. The second is the waste produced by repairs. The debris removal cost represents the cost to remove it from the site and dispose of it.

c) In addition, small losses can require special price considerations as average labor rate estimates may be inadequate. There are two general approaches to estimating the small job. One is to allow for driving time as well as time required to do the work. The more popular approach is to allow a minimum charge. The minimum charge quoted by a contractor usually represents two to four hours of labor and a small amount for materials.

There are many factors which determine costs. The following is a brief list of some of the common ones:

- Finance costs of construction
- Kind and quality of materials
- Difficulty of the job
- Work time overruns (overtime)
- Code requirements and regulations
- Quality workmanship
  (re-do work already completed)
- Accessibility to job site
  (material delivery, equipment transportation, narrow walkways, site on hill, etc.)
- Seasonal and current weather conditions
- Difficulty in material procurement
  (shortages in material needed, labor strikes, etc.)

Pricing Guidelines

There are various books currently published that simplify the process of establishing material costs, labor costs, unit costs and equipment costs. Some of these books can be very detailed and complex, while others are written from the layman's point of view and can easily be understood.

They offer information on which to base the cost factors of your project. They show a breakdown of pricing per unit and can be categorized by zip code to localize competitive pricing.

These books rely on historical pricing data concerning the various trades, and have been compiled and thoroughly analyzed by contractors who are well established within their trades, who have reputable backgrounds and are licensed, insured, and have expert knowledge in the applicable regulations of the trade.

One must be careful in selecting a price guide book. May of the books with which we are familiar deal with new construction and could be very inaccurate in pricing repairs. Generally speaking, a repair or restoration contractor must be very qualified in his/her work and completely aware of how to remove damaged items/areas. For example, not knowing how to remove damaged cabinets could cause unnecessary damage to adjacent drywall, electrical outlets and a myriad of circumstances. Similarly, an unqualified roofer that does an excellent job on new roofs may cause additional damage in repairing the same roof. By its very nature, re-construction is more time consuming and difficult than new construction. Some items of repair must be undone before they can be redone. "The Bluebook of Cleaning, Reconstruction and Repair Costs" is the standard in the industry and is one of the most accurate and reliable price guides on the market. It can be ordered directly from the publisher at (714) 731-3389 or fax at (714) 461-0049. By mail, send your correspondence c/o The Bluebook P.O. Box 5022-Y, Lake Forest, CA 92630. The cost is $64.95 and well worth it. You can also inquire at Barnes and Noble or your local library using ISBN #0-918767-00-8.

There is a special 50% discount coupon on page 160 for the Bluebook pricing guide.

Building Code Upgrade

Before you prepare your scope of repair it is very important to investigate two areas which may dramatically affect your final claim settlement. (1) Does your policy contain coverage for building code upgrade? (2) Are there state, city, municipal laws or regulations that directly affect repair or replacement to your residence?

The location of your residence can greatly impact the success of your property loss claim. For example, if your house is located in a fire severity zone (an area highly susceptible to fire outbreak) many cities require that when roof repair is in excess of a certain percentage of the entire roof, the material to be used in the repair or replacement must be upgraded to a fire rated material.

Building code upgrades can not only affect property in fire prone areas, it can also be required that upgrades be fulfilled in order to satisfy laws and regulations in areas prone to hurricanes, tornadoes, floods, and earthquakes.

Prior to preparing your scope of repair and subsequently submitting it to your insurance carrier you should do the following:

1. Review your policy. Some purchasers of property insurance are unaware of their coverages and entitlements regarding building code upgrade. You will generally find whether or not you are covered on the declaration page of your policy. Or, if you are uncertain, contact the insurance agent who sold you the policy.

   Where there appears to be an ambiguity in the language of the insurance policy concerning the availability of building code upgrade coverage, a recent California case, Mardirossian vs. Farmers Insurance Group, (May 29, 1997), Court of Appeal, Second District, Division 2 clarified any misunderstandings of the language contained in the policy in which your insurance carrier may be attempting to exclude building code upgrade coverage.

   In Mardisrossian, the insured did not have building code upgrade specifically set forth on the policy, but the court held that under a Guaranteed Replacement Cost Coverage policy building code upgrade could not be excluded because the language of the replacement guarantee policy was incompatible with this type of exclusion. In simple terms, if your policy does not specifically state that you possess building code upgrade, but you do possess a policy for Guaranteed Replacement, you may want to challenge your insurance carrier's position of exclusion by citing the Mardisrossian case.

2. Check with your local building department. Building codes are changing constantly and associated rules and regulations which may affect your property are subject to these changes. Contacting your city's building department and asking a question such as, "Has there been recent changes in requirements in my area which would affect repair or replacement to components of my home?"

   Remember building codes upgrades can require upgraded material replacement for all integral parts of your home including roofs, foundations, and structural components.

The reason for investigating this coverage in your policy is to eliminate any surprises that may await you after final settlement of your claim. If you hurriedly prepare your scope of repair, submit it to your insurance carrier, without including costs for code upgrade materials if applicable, you may be left paying out-of-pocket expenses to satisfy the state, city or municipal requirements of upgraded material long after you have concluded your claim with your insurance company.

RESTORATION CONTRACTOR'S ROLE

If you have retained a qualified restoration contractor to complete your work, and have assigned your claim to that contractor, then your loss situation should be in good hands. This is the ideal situation as the contractor should assume total responsibility from negotiations with the insurance company through complete restoration of your project.

The restoration contractor will usually supply and prepare all insurance forms for your convenience. You will be an integral part of making decisions and kept informed of any changes in the position of the insurance company. The restoration contractor's job is to keep you apprised of the progress of the work and he/she should see to it that your home is restored to the condition it was in before your loss.

MEASUREMENTS MADE EASY

A straight line is not a problem for most people, but various measurements which must be combined or calculated can sometimes be a little confusing. Accuracy is of primary importance because it determines how much material should be used with minimal waste.

MEASURING THE INTERIOR

Measuring a room with flat ceilings is straightforward. Simply multiply the Base times the Height to get the Area of the Wall.

Base (B) x Height (H) = Area

In the figure below, the formula is applied as follows:

20' x 8' = 160 sq. ft.   (sq. ft. = square feet)
It is true that rooms usually have four walls so just measure the base of all four walls and combine the totals.

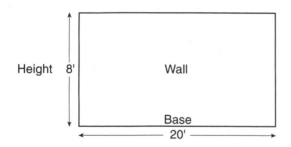

In the figure below, the room has two walls that are 20' x 8' and two walls that are 15' x 8'.

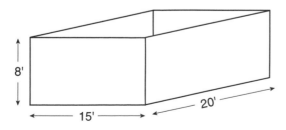

Apply the formula:

20' x 8' x 2 = 320 sq. ft.
15' x 8' x 2 = 240 sq. ft.

Total the Areas and the total wall area then becomes 560 sq. ft.

Use the same formula to measure the ceiling. It doesn't matter which is the base or height. If it is easier to visualize, use Width x Length = Area.

15' x 20' = 300 sq. ft. = Total Ceiling Area

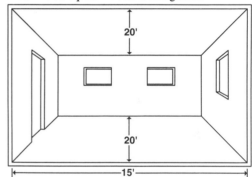

Floor Area = Ceiling Area = 15' x 20' = 300 sq. ft.

The Floor Area will be the same as the Ceiling Area in a room with flat ceilings. As the illustration above shows.

All rooms do not have flat ceilings. Some have vaulted or cathedral ceilings. Again, measure each wall separately.

Wall W is 16' x 20' = 320 sq. ft.
Wall Z is 8' x 20' = 160 sq. ft.

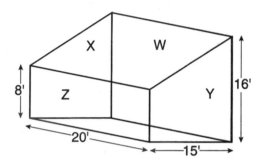

Wall X and Wall Y are the same size. Two steps are used to calculate the area. First, draw an imaginary line parallel to the base from the short side to the tall side. Notice that two shapes are formed.

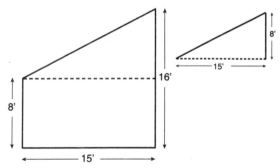

Second, apply the formula B x H = Area to the rectangle part. This is as follows:

15' x 8' = 120 sq. ft.
Then modify the formula for the triangle part as follows:

$1/2(B \times H) = 1/2 \times (15 \times 8) = $ Area
or $1/2 \times 120 = 60$ sq. ft.

Add the rectangle to the triangle
120 + 60 = 180 SF for Wall X & Wall Y.
Add all the walls together
320 + 180 + 180 + 160 = 840 sq. ft.

The long side of the triangle part is one side of the vaulted ceiling and is calculated as follows:

$8^2 + 15^2 = $ Long Side^2 or
64 + 225 = 289 then $\sqrt{289} = 17'$, so
17' x 20' = 340 sq. ft.

Add the walls and ceiling Area for a Total Area.
840 sq. ft. + 340 sq. ft. = 1180 sq. ft.

MEASURING THE EXTERIOR

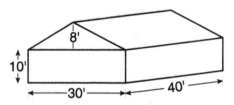

Measuring the exterior is the same process as the interior.

Two walls are 40' x 10' = 400 sq. ft. each.
Two walls are 30' x 10' = 300 sq. ft. each.
Two gables 1/2(30'x8') = 120 sq. ft. each.
Total 2 x (400 + 300 + 120) = 1640 sq. ft.

Roofing is measured similarly, but there is a specific standard unit of measure used.

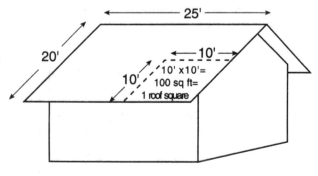

10' x 10' = 100 sq. ft.
This is equivalent to 1 Roofing Square.

ESTIMATING LINOLEUM

Estimating linoleum floors can be prone to inaccuracy, producing waste. Only when measurements are in even multiples of 6' or slightly less can estimates be accurate. Linoleum generally comes in 6' widths. A piece of linoleum is called a "drop" and, in this illustration, a piece of goods 6 x 20 or 120 sq. ft. is used for the installation.

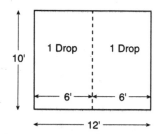

If we changed the dimensions of the room to 10 x 15 or 150 sq. ft., then 3 drops would be used producing 3' of waste.

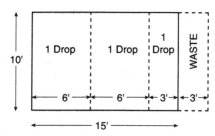

Cabinets, recesses and cutouts are represented in the illustration below. The drop on the left will require a 6' x 6' piece. The middle one will require a piece that is 6' x 10' and the one on the right will require a piece 6' x 10'4". This illustration will produce 2' x 10', 2' x3', and 1' x 1' waste.

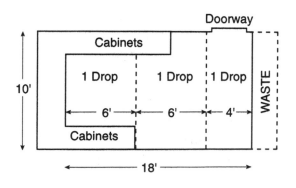

GEOMETRY LESSON

SQUARE: Square the length of one side.

$A = L^2$

RECTANGLE: Multiply length by width.
$A = LW$

TRIANGLE: Multiply half the altitude by the length of the base.
$A = AB/2$

CIRCLE: Square the diameter, and multiply by .7854.
$A = .7854D^2$

ELLIPSE: Multply the minor axis by the major axis by .7854.
$A = .7854Dd$

HEXAGON: Square the short diameter and multiply by .866, or square the long diameter and multiply by .6495.
$A = .866d^2$, or $A = .6495D^2$

OCTAGON: Square the diameter and multiply by .828, or square the long diameter and multiply by .707.
$A = .828d^2$, or $A = .707D^2$

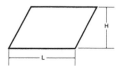

PARALLELOGRAM: Multiply length by perpendicular height.
$A = LH$

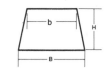

TRAPEZOID: Multiply height by half the sum of the top and bottom bases.
$A = H(b+B)/2$

SAMPLE JOB - "SCOPE OF REPAIRS"

Scenario:

During the night, there was a heavy wind and rain storm. The wind blew many shingles off the roof. The rain water came into the house through the holes in the roof. It damaged the insulation in the attic, the living room ceiling, walls and carpet.

NOTE: Each incident gives rise to unique circumstances for which the following drafts may or may not be appropriate. You need to carefully review the extent of your damage and perform a thorough investigation to determine the scope, breakdown and cost of each line item repair.

FORMS
FORMS
FORMS
FORMS

THERE ARE FORMS IN CHAPTER 16 FOR YOU TO USE AND MODIFY DEPENDING ON THE NATURE OF YOUR CLAIM.

SCOPE OF REPAIRS

INSURED: MR. HOMEOWNER

ADDRESS: 2200 Anystreet

CITY STATE ZIP: Any City U.S.A 92000

H/PH:

B/PH:

INSURANCE CO.: Any Homeowner Insurance Co

POLICY #: My Policy no

CLAIM #: My Claim no.

DATE OF LOSS: February 3, 0000

TYPE OF LOSS: Wind/Water

AREA NAME: Roof   AREA DIMENSIONS: 30' x 20'   PG 1 OF 3

DESCRIPTION	#/U	U/M	PPU	COST
During the night, the wind and rain storm blew about 10-15% of the wood shingles off of one side of the roof, including ridge caps and field shingles. The next day, an emergency cover was put on the roof to mitigate further damage to the interior.				
It has been determined by a roofing contractor that due to the extent of the damage and to make a proper repair, the rest of the shingles have to be removed and replaced.				
The following is the determined scope of repairs and cost estimate:				
emergency roof cover-up		per invoice		$300.00
city permit for roof work				$175.00
trash bin rental for debris removal	1	wk	175.00	$175.00
demo existing wood shingles	6	sq	50.00	$300.00
material and labor for wood shingles in field	6	sq	300.00	1,800.00
install ridge caps	30	ft	6.00/ft	$180.00
final clean-up and debris removal	2	hr	$30.00	$60.00
		total roof repairs		$2,990.00

SCOPE OF REPAIRS

INSURED: MR. Homeowner

ADDRESS: 2200 AnyStreet

CITY STATE ZIP: Any City U.S.A 92000

H/PH:

B/PH:

INSURANCE CO.: Any Homeowner Insurance Co

POLICY #: My Policy no

CLAIM #: My Claim no.

DATE OF LOSS: February 3, 0000

TYPE OF LOSS: Wind/Water

AREA NAME: Living Room   **AREA DIMENSIONS:** 15' x 20' x 8' high   PG 2 OF 3

When the shingles blew off the Roof, Rainwater entered into the house through the holes in the Roof; damaging the ceiling, walls and carpet. The next day, a water removal company extracted the water from the carpet. The following is the determined scope of Repairs with the cost estimates:

DESCRIPTION	#/U	U/M	PPU	COST
water Removal	SEE INVOICE			$200.00
asbestos test of acoustical ceiling materials				$75.00
move furniture	2	hr	30	$60.00
mask off Room to isolate work area	2	hr	30	$60.00
1 mil plastic	1	Roll	15	$15.00
scrape entire ceiling	300	sfc	.26	$78.00
drywall Repair to ceiling	min	chg		$375.00
paint to seal ceiling bleed through	300	sfc	.45	$135.00
Reapply acoustical ceiling material	300	sfc	.66	$198.00
paint walls 2 coats	720	sfw	.46	$331.20
paint windows	3x4' 2	ea	21.00	$42.00
paint doors	2	ea	18.50	#37.00
paint base boards	87	lft	1.35	$117.45
clean, disinfect, & deodorize carpet	300	sff	.32	$96.00
Replace furniture	2	hr	30.00	$60.00
final cleanup	2	hr	30.00	$60.00
			total living Room	$1,939.65

LEGEND							
AMP-Amperes	CFDAY-Cost/CF/Day	EST-Estimated Amount	LF-Lineal Feet	PR-Pair	SFF-Sq Foot of Floor	SYF-Sq Yd Floor	U/M-Unit of Measure
AVG-Average	CY-Cubic Yards	H-Height	LI-Lineal Inch	R&R-Remove/Replace/Reset	SFW-Sq Foot of Walls	SYL-Sq Yd Linoleum	V-Volts
BINS-No. of Bins	D-Depth	HRS-No. of Hours	L/M-Labor& Materials	S/C-Service Charge	SQ-Square of Roofing	SYW-Sq Yd Walls	W-Wide
CF-Cubic Feet	EA-Each Unit	LDS-No. of Loads	M/C-Minimum Charge	SF-Square Feet	SY-Square Yard	T&G-Tongue & Groove	TK/D-Truck Loads per Day
			PPU-Price per Unit	SFC-Sq Foot Ceiling	SYC-Sq Yd Ceiling		#/U-No. of Units

SCOPE OF REPAIRS

INSURED MR. HOMEOWNER

ADDRESS 2200 Anystreet

CITY STATE ZIP Any City U.S.A 92000

H/PH

B/PH

INSURANCE CO. Any Homeowner Insurance Co

POLICY # My Policy no

CLAIM # My Claim no.

DATE OF LOSS February 3, 0000

TYPE OF LOSS Wind/Water

AREA NAME

AREA DIMENSIONS

PG. 3 OF 3

DESCRIPTION	#/U	U/M	PPU	COST
total Roof Repairs page 1				$2,990.00
total living Room Repairs page 2				$1,939.65
total Repairs				$4,929.65
If a contractor is used to perform the work, then the contractor is entitled (generally) to an additional 10% overhead (OH) and 10% profit (P).				
10% OH				$492.97
10% P				$492.97
total loss claimed				$5,915.59
less deductible				$ 200.00
net claim				$5,715.59

CHAPTER 9

NEGOTIATING THE CLAIM

- **WHO IS BEST TO NEGOTIATE YOUR CLAIM?**
  YOU, A PUBLIC ADJUSTER, A RESTORATION CONTRACTOR OR AN ATTORNEY?

- **YOUR POSITION**

- **THE INSURANCE COMPANY'S POSITION**

- **UNFAIR CLAIMS SETTLEMENT PRACTICES ACT**

- **YOUR RIGHTS AND OBLIGATIONS**

- **THE ART OF NEGOTIATION**

By this time, you have maintained your claims file and have gathered information, documentation and evidence pertaining to your loss and photographs needed to assess the value of your claim. Your preparation of the materials needed for claims submission and the knowledge you gained in the preceding chapters should minimize your anxiety prior to your bout in the negotiation arena. Maintain a firm but flexible position, listen intently to what the adjuster says, and counter with your own demand for settlement. You are prepared - don't weaken.

WHO IS BEST TO NEGOTIATE YOUR CLAIM ?

You, a Public Adjuster, a Restoration Contractor or an Attorney?

You:

If you are not experienced in dealing with an insurance company, it can be an exercise in frustration and futility. Claims offices work with paper and numbers and, once you are into the system, it can be either a pleasant experience or a journey into the unknown.

After you submit your documentation and other forms of evidence to support your claim, you may encounter an insurance adjuster whose personal agenda is to settle your claim for the minimum amount that can be compromised.

You may or may not have a flexible enough schedule to make on-site inspection appointments, participate in negotiation discussions, prepare additional evidence submissions, etc., and yet once the insurance company develops a file on your claim, their goal is to resolve the claim. If this is done too swiftly, you may be unprepared or, worse than that, cause your claim to be undervalued.

Some of the intricacies of your policy will be completely foreign to you, and confusion on other matters may make your claims experience frustrating and unsettling.

If you decide that you need help in processing your own claim, you have three additional choices. They are the public adjuster, the restoration contractor or an attorney.

The Public Adjusters:

No other class of adjuster is more at odds with insurance companies than the public adjuster.

The simple reason is that too many times an unscrupulous public adjuster or marketer will do anything in order to be retained. Some of these unethical public adjusters will attempt to lure the insured away from the control of their claim and settle the matter quickly without regard for the true valuation of the claim.

The majority of public adjusters are decent individuals devoted to providing assistance to insureds that find themselves unable, for whatever reason, to process and negotiate an insurance claim. A typical example of this is when the insurance company will offer very little to the insured at which time the public adjuster will be retained to handle the claims process on behalf of the insured. The public adjuster's fee range from 10%-12% of the recovery of the claim.

Before engaging a public adjuster you should inquire as to his or her experience in the insurance field and their prior involvement with your insurance carrier and weigh the advantages the public adjuster has against your experience with the handling of an insurance claim.

A public adjuster, however, is not always necessary. Many claims are simple to resolve, but if more money is involved in a claim or if the complexities of the claim require expertise you are not familiar with, then a public adjuster is needed.

You can always just consult with a public adjuster, and continue handling your claim yourself. If your claim becomes confusing or involved you can always retain the public adjuster to assist you.

In California, as in most states, public adjusters are licensed by the Department of Insurance. Public adjusters can only solicit business between the hours of 8:00 a.m. and 6:00 p.m., seven days a week.

Your contract with a public adjuster is subject to a three (3) day notice of recession, which means you have three days or seventy-two (72) hours to accept the terms of the public adjuster's contract or rescind your contract. Always check your state's laws before signing a contract with a public adjuster.

The Restoration Contractor:

Perhaps your best choice is the qualified restoration contractor because he/she is primarily involved in day to day contact with insurance companies negotiating and adjusting property claims. Their expertise in this field far surpasses any individual or business entity holding themselves out to represent your claim on a one time basis.

A good restoration contractor has expertise, not only in the construction industry and all of the related trades, they are also experts in the complexities and details required in handling a property insurance claim. They know the "territory," negotiation techniques, and the value of claims and settlements. Small details, which you may overlook, are covered by the competency of a qualified restoration contractor.

When you choose a good qualified restoration contractor and assign your claim to him or her, he/she should provide the service of processing, handling and monitoring your claim from submission to settlement. You can look forward to quality service, both in restoration and in claims processing, without the additional burden of out-of-pocket expenses to someone charging a fee to process your claim.

The restoration of your property should begin swiftly and be completed by a competent, bonded, licensed and insured restoration contractor. Your claims file will be monitored by the insurance processing unit of the restoration contactor, and you will benefit from the peace of mind that you have made a wise choice.

The Attorney:

All claims are unique in their make-up and character. If your claim is one involving large sums of money or the complexities of the claim seem overwhelming, you might consider having an experienced attorney handle the negotiation phase of the process.

Finding an attorney who specializes in the field of property claims can sometimes be a difficult task, since negotiating of homeowner's property damage claim requires a thorough knowledge of the construction trade. Even competent attorneys will sometimes seek the advice and direction of a contractor in evaluating and assessing the final demand for settlement.

Also, remember that attorneys seldom charge a flat fee for their services. They are more apt to be retained either on a contingency basis (charging a percentage of your final settlement) or on an hourly basis.

The services of an attorney can be invaluable if your claim is at an impasse with the insurance company or if you foresee a possible action of bad faith, misrepresentation or fraud committed by your insurance company.

YOUR POSITION

When you find yourself in a situation that requires filing an insurance claim, you will quickly realize that the world of policy contracts and claims handling is a confusing and complex one. Advertisers and insurance salespeople frequently imply that filing a claim is an effortless and satisfactory experience. In fact, it is usually somewhat difficult, and can be more like a tax audit than anything else. Your initial inclination may be to rely on your insurance agent for assistance, but you will probably discover that most insurance agents have a limited knowledge of claims processing. However, they can become helpful in contacting claims supervisors or managers if you are having a difficult time with an adjuster, especially if you are a long time insured.

By approaching the insurance claim process with a pragmatic attitude, creativity, common sense and a willingness to become involved in the situation, it is possible for you to affect the outcome of the claim a great deal.

THE INSURANCE COMPANY'S POSITION

The company must first honor its obvious obligations under the policy contract. Then, the insurance company is expected to interpret the policy, when necessary, in a manner consistent with case and statutory law.

A basic point to keep in mind is that insurance companies are different, and each has its own unique personality. Company policy on claims handling varies considerably. Many carriers bend over backwards to find justification in covering losses. If it is possible to find a line of reasoning which enables coverage to be extended to a loss, these carriers will provide coverage.

Approaches to claims, however, are sometimes based on arbitrary company policies that are not in keeping with standard practices and legal rules. At times, incorrect decisions are made by insurance company personnel who aren't knowledgeable and unfortunately, sometimes unscrupulous practices are unknowingly followed.

Some companies work tirelessly to minimize payments and to deny as many claims as possible. These companies usually adopt positions on questionable claims which are contrary to the interest of their customers, deciding every issue against the policyholder. Some companies may go so far as to engage in business practices which are not only unfair, but may be illegal as well. Such companies, fortunately, represent a small minority, but they do exist.

UNFAIR CLAIMS SETTLEMENT PRACTICES ACT

To further protect your rights, most states have now adopted a model of the Unfair Claims Settlement Practices Act, which are laws passed by state legislatures to regulate the behavior of insurance companies with respect to the payment of claims.

The statutes primarily regulate the treatment of policyholders and claimants. The requirements are usually not more than a couple of pages long and are usually clearly written and easily understood. The content of these statutes varies from state to state although most are similar in actual requirements. A copy of the Unfair Claims Settlement Practices Act that applies in your state can be obtained from your State Insurance Commissioner's Office (see Chapter 9 - "State Listings").

The following is the current California Unfair Claims Settlement Practices Act:

Section 790.03(h)—Knowingly committing or performing with such frequency as to indicate a general business practice any of the following unfair claims practices:

(1) Misrepresenting to claimants pertinent facts or insurance policy provisions relating to any coverage at issue.

(2) Failing to acknowledge and act reasonably promptly upon communications with respect to claims arising under insurance policies.

(3) Failing to adopt and implement reasonable standards for the prompt investigation and processing of claims arising under insurance policies.

(4) Failing to affirm or deny coverage of claims within a reasonable time after proof of loss requirements have been completed and submitted by the insured.

(5) Not attempting in good faith to effectuate prompt, fair and equitable settlements of claims in which liability has become reasonably clear.

(6) Compelling insureds to institute litigation to recover amounts due under an insurance policy by offering substantially less than the amounts ultimately recovered in actions brought by such insureds.

(7) Attempting to settle a claim by an insured for less than the amount to which a reasonable man would have believed he was entitled by reference to written or printed advertising material accompanying or made part of an application.

(8) Attempting to settle claims on the basis of an application which was altered without notice to, or knowledge or consent of, the insured, his representative, agent or broker.

(9) Failing, after payment of a claim, to inform insureds or beneficiaries upon request by them, of the coverage under which payment has been made.

(10) Making known to insureds or claimants a practice of the insurer of appealing from arbitration awards in favor of insureds or claimants for the purpose of compelling them to accept settlements or compromises less than the amount awarded in arbitration.

(11) Delaying the investigation or payment of claims by requiring an insured, claimant, or the physician of either, to submit a preliminary claim report, and then requiring the subsequent submission of formal proof of loss forms, both of which submissions contain substantially the same information.

(12) Failing to settle claims promptly, where liability has become apparent, under one portion of the insurance policy coverage in order to influence settlement under other portions of the insurance policy coverage.

(13) Failing to provide promptly a reasonable explanation of the basis relied on in the insurance policy, in relation to the facts or applicable law, for the denial of a claim or for the offer of a compromise settlement.

(14) Directly advising a claimant not to obtain the services of an attorney.

(15) Misleading a claimant as to the applicable statute of limitations.

YOUR RIGHTS AND OBLIGATIONS

As the policyholder, only you can make sure that your insurance company lives up to its obligations under the policy/contract. It is recommended that you do so based on a strong conviction that fair dealing, quality workmanship and ethical business practices benefit the insurance industry just as they benefit the public. Your homeowners insurance policy is a contract between you and a financial institution that is not in the emergency service business. The contract entitles you to certain rights and imposes obligations on both you and your insurance company.

- You may obtain emergency services to safeguard your property from further damage after a loss, and you may be fully compensated for the cost of such services. In fact, after a loss, you have the <u>obligation</u> to safeguard (mitigate) your property from further damage. Your insurance company may not be liable for additional expense if you fail to provide such protection. This is called mitigating your damages.

- You have the right to have a professional loss consultant, i.e., public adjuster, lawyer, etc., represent your interests and guide you in the presentation of your claim to the insurance company's adjusters (at your expense).

- If you have secured adequate coverage, you should be entitled to be paid for the market value of fully restoring your property to its pre-damaged condition. However, you are not insured for the repair of unrelated problems, code deficiencies or prior damage.

- You are entitled to employ a full-time restoration professional who is licensed, insured, of good reputation, and can demonstrate his/her capabilities, availability, skill and experience in insurance damage repair.

- The repair contract and its performance is strictly between you and the contractor. Generally, your insurance company does not warrant or guarantee the performance of any firm you hire. So be sure to have the contractor put any agreement into writing.

- You are entitled to materials and workmanship fully equivalent to your existing installation in like kind and quality. The insurance company has no obligation to improve your existing installation.

- You are not required to accept the lowest bidder. Nowhere in your policy do the words "cheapest," "low" or "low price" appear. However, repair rates should correspond to prevailing standards in your area for work of good quality.

- Before work begins, you are entitled to receive from both the adjuster and contractor, a detailed listing of the scope of repairs and quantities of materials to be provided. Provisions for hidden or latent problems relating to the damage should also be spelled out in as much detail as possible.

- You are entitled to a contract that provides all federal, state and local requirements for construction work. However, you must be familiar with these requirements in order to enjoy the protection the law provides. Ask your State License Board or the Department of Consumer Affairs for this important information.

- If there is a disagreement between you and the insurance company which cannot be resolved, you are entitled to request arbitration and/or appraisal subject to the terms of your policy. The standard policy spells out the procedures for settling differences without resorting to a lawsuit.

- The insurance company must pay you within the time specified in the contract. State insurance regulations vary with respect to the time requirements. The "time" clause is designed to prevent insurance companies from using delay and/or personal hardship as a tactic to compel a lower settlement. However, the policy also has time requirements for you, the policyholder, within which you must prepare and submit your "Proof of Loss." Know about these in advance so that you can be in compliance.

The Art of Negotiation

Negotiating a settlement with an insurance adjuster demands a business-like attitude and a good understanding of the claims process. And, of course, it takes preparation. To prepare for such negotiations there are three things to remember: know your rights, have thorough documentation, and be able to verify your claim. By being prepared in this way your negotiating skills will be utilized most effectively.

The dynamics of good negotiation are characterized by six interrelated elements; preparation, common sense, objectivity, principle, communication, and compromise.

Preparation is a must! Have all your documentation close at hand in order to substantiate your claim.

Common sense or good sound judgment will always be your best ally. Recognize what is relevant vs. irrelevant, material vs. immaterial, fact vs. fiction.

Be objective. Objectivity is the concentrated effort to see things clearly and without bias or prejudice. By being objective you can easily identify whether the adjuster's statements are made in good faith. How do you maintain this objectivity? The most effective way is by sticking to the relevant issues of the claim, recognizing how your views are similar or dissimilar to the adjuster's, avoiding the sway of emotion or pressure, not relying on unsubstantiated statements, and verifying the adjuster's statements through qualified sources.

At times it can be very challenging to maintain an objective attitude while negotiating. Your objectivity will be borne out by your open-mindedness toward the issues and your ability to recognize the adjuster's perspective.

When settling your claim use a principled approach. Be sure the adjuster is maintaining the professional standards his/her company advertises. Be straight-forward in your communications and do not become emotionally affected by unreasonable assertions. Never yield to pressure, intimidation, evasion or unreasonable negotiation procedures.

Effective communication is a product of accessibility, having a positive attitude, and concentration. Accessibility is maintained by first finding out the adjuster's daily routine. Adjuster's work schedules are open. They do not punch a time-clock and are usually available at any reasonable hour. Speak optimistically as though your every statement is simply a breath away from happening. Show confidence, carry a look of success, and espouse an attitude that the claim will be resolved only through fairness, honesty and reasonableness.

Don't be afraid to ask questions.

STATE LISTINGS of DEPARTMENTS of INSURANCE

The following is a list of the individual states and phone numbers of their respective offices for the Department of Insurance as well as each state's adoption of legislation regarding Unfair Claims Settlement Practices Act. It is important that you contact your own state's individual Department of Insurance Office in order to obtain updated information and legislation enactments that may govern claims for your particular insurance matter.

STATE	PHONE	MODEL/SIMILAR LEGISLATION
Alabama	(334) 269-3550	NO ACTION TO DATE
Alaska	(907) 269-7900	ALASKA STAT. §§ 21.36.125 (1976) (1)
Arizona	(602) 912-8400	ARIZ. REV. STAT. ANN. § 20-461 (1981/1991) (1)
Arkansas	(501) 371-2600 (800) 852-5494 (Hotline)	ARK. STAT. ANN. § 23-66-206 (1959/1987) (1)
California	(916) 445-5544 (800) 927-4357 (Hotline)	CAL. INS. CODE § 790.03 (1959/1989) (1)
Colorado	(303) 894-7499 Ext. 311	COLO. REV. STAT. § 10-3-1104 (1963/1989) (1)
Connecticut	(203) 297-3800	CONN. GEN. STAT. § 38a-816 (1955/1989) (1)
Delaware	(302) 739-4251	DEL. INS. REG. 26 (1977) (1)
D.C.	(202) 727-8000	NO ACTION TO DATE
Florida	(904) 922-3100 (800) 342-2762 (Hotline)	FLA. STAT. § 626.9541 (1976/1990) (1)
Georgia	(404) 656-2056	GA. CODE. ANN. §§ 33-6-30 to 33-6-37 (1992) (2)
Guam	011 (671) 475-5000	NO ACTION TO DATE
Hawaii	(808) 586-2790	HAWAII REV. STAT. § 431:13-103 (1988/1989) (1)
Idaho	(208) 334-4250	IDAHO CODE §§ 41-1329 (1977/1987) (1)
Illinois	(217) 782-4515	NO ACTION TO DATE
Indiana	(317) 232-2385 (800) 622-4461 (Hotline)	IND. CODE § 27-4-1-4.5 (1983/1987) (1)
Iowa	(515) 281-5705	NO ACTION TO DATE
Kansas	(913) 296-3071 (800) 432-2484 (Hotline)	KAN. STAT. ANN. §§ 40-2404 (1955/1992) (1)
Kentucky	(502) 564-6027	KY. REV. STAT. §§ 304.12-230 (1984/1988) (1)
Louisiana	(504) 342-5900	LA. REV. STAT. ANN. § 22:1214 (1958/1989) (1) Related Legislation - LA. REV. STAT. ANN. § 22:1220 (1990) (duty of P/C

insurers).

STATE	PHONE	MODEL/SIMILAR LEGISLATION
Maine	(207) 624-8475 (800) 300-5000 (Hotline)	ME. REV. STAT. ANN. tit. 24-A § 2164-D (1987) (Part of model) (1)
Maryland	(410) 333-2521 (800) 492-6116 (Hotline)	MD. ANN. CODE art. 48A § 230A (1986) (1)
Massachusetts	(617) 521-7794 (617) 521-7777 (Hotline)	MASS. GEN. LAWS ch. 176D § 3 (1972/1986) (1)
Michigan	(517) 373-9273	MICH. COMP. LAWS § 500.2026 (1951/1977) (1)
Minnesota	(612) 296-6848	MINN. STAT. § 72A.20 Sub. 12 (1967/1986) (1)
Mississippi	(601) 359-3569 (800) 562-2957	NO ACTION TO DATE
Missouri	(573) 751-4126 (800) 726-7390 (Hotline)	MO. REV. STAT. §§ 375.1000 to 375.1018 (1991/1993) (2)
Montana	(406) 444-2040 (800) 332-6148 (Hotline)	MONT. CODE ANN. § 33-18-201 (1977) (1)
Nebraska	(402) 471-2201	NEB. REV. STAT. §§ 44-1536 to 44-1544 (1991/1994) (2)
Nevada	(702) 687-4270 (800) 992-0900 (Hotline)	NEV. REV. STAT. § 686A.310 (1975/1987) (1)
New Hampshire	(603) 271-2261	N.H. REV. STAT. ANN. § 417:4 (1947/1991) (1)
New Jersey	(609) 292-5363	N.J. REV. STAT. § 17:29B-4 (1947/1975) (1)
New Mexico	(505) 827-4601 (800) 947-4722 (Hotline)	N.M. STAT. ANN. § 59A-16-20 (1985/1993) (1)
New York	(212) 602-0429 (800) 342-3736	N.Y. INS.LAW § 2601 (1984) (1)
North Carolina	(919) 733-7349 (800) 662-7777 (Hotline)	N.C. GEN. STAT. § 58-63-15 (1949/1987) (1)
North Dakota	(701) 328-2440 (800) 247-0560 (Hotline)	N.D. CENT. CODE §§ 26.1-04-03 (1983/1989) (1)
Ohio	(614) 644-2658 (800) 686-1526 (Hotline)	OHIO INS. REG. RULE 3901-1-07 (1975) (1)
Oklahoma	(405) 521-2828 (800) 522-0071 (Hotline)	Related legislation - OKLA. STAT. tit. 36 §§ 1251 to 1260 (1986/1994).
Oregon	(503) 378-4271	OR. REV. STAT. § 746.230 (1967/1989) (1)
Pennsylvania	(717) 783-0442	PA. CONS. STAT. § 40-29-105 (1974/1984) (1)

STATE	PHONE	MODEL/SIMILAR LEGISLATION
Puerto Rico	(787) 722-8686	P.R. LAWS ANN. tit. 26 § 2716a (1974) (1)
Rhode Island	(401) 277-2223	R.I. GEN. LAWS §§ 29-9.1-1 to 29-9.1-9 (1993).
South Carolina	(803) 737-6160	S.C. CODE ANN. §§ 38-59-10 to 38-59-50 (1987) (Model and more) (1)
South Dakota	(605) 773-3563 (605) 773-3563 (Hotline)	S.D. CODIFIED LAWS ANN. § 58-33-67 (1986/1989) (1)
Tennessee	(615) 741-2241 (800) 342-4029 (Hotline)	TENN. CODE ANN. § 56-8-104 (1981/1989) (1)
Texas	(512) 463-6169 (800) 578-4677 (Hotline)	TEX. ADMIN. REGS. § 21.203 (1976/1985) (1) Related legislation - TEX. INS. CODE ANN. art. 21.55 (1991).
Utah	(801) 538-3800 (800) 439-3805 (Hotline)	UTAH CODE ANN. §§ 31A-26-303 to 31A-26-310 (1986) (1)
Vermont	(802) 828-3301	VT. STAT. ANN. tit. 8 § 4724 (1955/1987) (1)
Virgin Islands	(809) 773-6449	NO ACTION TO DATE
Virginia	(804) 371-9741 (800) 552-7945 (Hotline)	VA. CODE §§ 38.2-510 (1986/1988) (1) Related legislation - See Also: VA. CODE § 38.2-517 (1992
Washington	(360) 753-7300 (800) 562-6900 (Hotline)	WASH. ADMIN. CODE R. § 284-30-330 (1978/1987) (1)
West Virginia	(304) 558-3386 (800) 642-9004 (Hotline)	W. VA. CODE § 33-11-4 (1957/1985) (1)
Wisconsin	(608) 266-3586 (800) 236-8517 (Hotline)	WIS. ADMIN. CODE § 6.11 (1971/1992) (1)
Wyoming	(307) 777-7401 (800) 438-5768 (Hotline)	WYO. STAT. § 26-13-124 (1986) (1)

NOTE: For more information on the "UNFAIR CLAIMS SETTLEMENT PRACTICES ACT" including recent changes, modifications, case law, legislative history, and regulation updates, contact the National Association of Insurance Commissioners (NAIC), Publications Department, Support & Services Office at:
120 W. Twelfth Street, Ste. 1100, Kansas City, MO 64105-1925 (816) 842-3600 or (816) 374-7259

CHAPTER 10

THE ADJUSTER

- **ROLE OF THE ADJUSTER**

- **INVESTIGATION**

- **EVALUATION**

- **TYPES OF ADJUSTERS**

- **DEALING WITH TROUBLESOME ADJUSTERS**

- **KNOW THE GAMES SOME ADJUSTERS PLAY**

- **INSURANCE COMPANY CHAIN OF COMMAND**

ROLE OF THE ADJUSTER

The responsibilities of handling your insurance claim are the same regardless of what type of adjuster your insurance company uses. Some companies may even use both a staff adjuster and an independent adjuster to process your claim.

The adjuster's primary task is to provide assistance and service to the insured so that covered claims are paid promptly. This may be accomplished by payment of the full amount demanded, or by negotiating a settlement. The claims adjuster employs two steps to accomplish this purpose.

INVESTIGATION

This procedure consists of a reasonable inquiry into the facts of the loss to determine whether coverage applies. Since adjusters are rarely eyewitnesses to the loss, they must rely upon secondary evidence such as statements from the insured and a survey of the premises and debris to make their determination.

EVALUATION

Having conducted the investigation and determined the amount of damage, the claims adjuster can then make an approximation of the value of the claim, so that the proper amount can be paid for repairs.

The adjuster will need to work closely with the insurance company's experts and your experts, such as contractors and architects, to provide an accurate evaluation.

It is important that you make contact with your assigned adjuster as soon as possible so that the claim process can begin. You should also remain in contact with your adjuster on a regular basis to ensure that your claim is still on track and so that any questions or concerns you may have can be answered and resolved.

Your adjuster is responsible for monitoring and guiding your claim to its conclusion. It is important that the adjuster be advised of any changes made in your home design, or any other significant action by you, your contractor or other representative. This will minimize any miscommunication and help to keep your claim on track.

TYPES OF ADJUSTERS

When your claim is assigned to an adjuster, you, as the claimant, have little choice as to who is appointed to work with you. You may have to deal with an individual who is openly aggressive, or you may have the pleasure of working with an individual who is compassionate and understanding.

Throughout the insurance industry, the majority of people that you will deal with, from agency representatives to claims office management, are dedicated employees who must maintain an even balance between the economic interest of the company and the servicing of the company's insured's claims and inquiries.

Adjusters are often rated by their supervisors on the basis of performance. The more money saved, the higher the rating. Evaluations are based on the difference between the amount of the claim and the amount of the final settlement. It is evident, under such circumstances, why an adjuster would never advise an insured that he is entitled to a higher settlement. His rating would suffer!

Whatever type of adjuster you encounter, remember that all businesses have good people and all businesses, unfortunately, have a few that are difficult to deal with.

Insurance Company Adjusters:

Insurance company adjusters are your most commonly encountered adjusters. They are hired, trained and paid by the insurance companies. These adjusters are the unsung heroes of the insurance community. They are typically overworked and underpaid, which explains their high turnover rate. The major insurance companies employ company trained adjusters and place them in strategically located areas to service their policyholders with their claims. Insurance company adjusters reflect a wide divergence of experience and expertise among adjusters. You will find the very best and the very worst of adjusters in this category. You will find that your very best efforts at diplomacy will be required of you, if you are assigned an inexperienced adjuster.

Independent Adjusters:

Another type of adjuster that you may encounter is the independent adjuster. An independent adjuster is independent from any insurance company. He/she can be associated with a specific group of experienced adjusters, or simply an individual that has established his/her own business who services established insurance companies. The companies who call on the services of an independent adjuster may be a major insurance company who is overloaded with claims and sends their excess claims out to independents, or it may be an out-of-state insurance company that has no claims office in the area. In this case, the insurance company will call the independent adjuster out on a loss and the independent adjuster will handle the claim for a fee. You are likely to find your most experienced and "savvy" adjusters within this category. They have paid their dues by working for an established insurance company and are now out on their own. There is not enough wool in the world that one can use to pull over their eyes. Their loyalty is to the insurance company that hired them. This does not mean that they will not ever see your point of view if a difference arises, but it does mean that the independent adjuster is more likely to side with the insurance company who hired him in such disputes, even more than with the homeowner. The reason for this is obvious: It is the insurance company who will hire him/her again if they are confident in their abilities and "fairness." Fairness can be interpreted from many different perspectives and angles. It just depends on your vantage point.

DEALING WITH TROUBLESOME ADJUSTERS

Troublesome adjusters can appear in just about any situation during the claims process. It may be that the person you are dealing with has a brash personality or maybe he/she is just having a "bad day."

Most adjusters that you encounter are upstanding, fair and ethical individuals who have a true concern about your loss with the main objective of restoring your property. But some can create real problems and consume your time, energy and efforts.

You may meet the adjuster who is primarily operating under his or her own agenda. That is, they possess an arrogance about themselves as a result of the position they hold or the personality they have developed. This type of individual will make deliberate attempts to confuse and confound you and may even be trying to thwart the progress of your claim for their own specific reasons. It may be they are overwhelmed by their workload, or just feel that intimidating claimants lessens their efforts in adjusting claims.

Be aware that this type of troublesome adjuster may either show up too early or too late for a scheduled on-site inspection to catch you "off guard." This tactic is sometimes deployed to make sure your contractor or some other advisor is not in attendance when the adjuster arrives. These troublesome adjusters tend to have overt characteristic traits which may be indicated by the following:

- Intimidating remarks as to the cause and coverage of your loss.

- A suspicious attitude of the reason you are filing a loss claim.

- Being accusatory toward you - "Didn't you help create this situation?"

- "Low-Balling" the settlement amount.

- Delaying the claims process.

- Not returning calls or inquiries.

- Unethically pressuring you to use his or her contractor to do your repair work.

These types of red flags should give you an indication that you are dealing with a troublesome adjuster. Sometimes just by communicating with the adjuster, you may find that he or she may be overworked, frustrated in their position, "climbing the corporate ladder" or operating outside of the insurance company's service policies.

Even inexperienced adjusters can be categorized as troublesome at times. Sometimes their case workloads exceed their ability to manage such volume of work, or their lack of knowledge translates into an arrogant attitude of defensiveness rather that empathy toward the claimant.

If problems continue to persist between you and the claims adjuster, start with calling the claims office and ask to speak to the adjuster's supervisor. In most cases, this is all that will be necessary. Candidly and politely explain to the supervisor your problem. Tell him/her that you have already made a number of calls to the adjuster with no response and that you are perplexed as to why. Further explain that the repairs to your dwelling are being delayed as a result, because the contractor has stated that the repairs to your dwelling cannot commence or proceed until you and the adjuster work out your differences.

If your call to the supervisor results in the supervisor doing nothing more than supporting the adjusters position, immediately write a letter to the claims manager (see Chapter 15 "Form Letters") and send a "cc" copy to the Vice-President of the Insurance Company.

In any situation, be sure to completely document any and all conversations. Have any adjuster who denies coverage put their denial in writing! This is what they are required to do. Also, document the damages thoroughly and keep complete records of everything! You should also take note that if you are faced with a troublesome adjuster this is probably the appropriate time to begin to consider going up the chain of command and solicit the assistance of someone at a higher level of management. If necessary, do not hesitate to utilize the chain of command and to inform the upper management of the company of your grievances and ask for their intervention (see Chapter 10 - "Chain of Command").

KNOW THE GAMES SOME ADJUSTERS PLAY

Researchers preparing for this book conducted a survey among ex-insurance adjusters, ex-insurance supervisors, and ex-insurance claims managers which provided an interesting view of what some insurance representatives will do to stall or delay your efforts in filing a claim.

Most insurance representatives that possess an overzealous attitude are simply on a "power trip" and are too difficult to deal with. Your insurance company can normally "weed out" the overzealous adjuster from the mainstream of customer service and eventually reassign the adjuster to another division of claims or even terminate their service.

However, the adjuster that remains on the job can create problems also. The trouble soon appears when your calls go unreturned. The overzealous adjusters are "notoriously" known throughout the industry. Homeowners, contractors, attorneys and even insurance companies have trouble with this type of adjuster.

A large majority of homeowners placing claims for property damage encounter difficult adjusters. Look for the following list of indicators to alert you that it is now time to either request a change in adjusters or go up the chain of command in the claims office to get the response you are entitled to as an insured.

- Non-responsive to telephone calls.
- "Your file is lost."
- "I never received your mail."
- "I never received your fax."
- "Your estimate is miles apart from my evaluation."
- "I sent you a letter, didn't you receive it?"
- "My supervisor is on vacation."
- "I have not been given any authority to settle your claim yet."
- "I'll be tied up for the next couple of weeks."
- "I'll have to request your file from the home office. It might take some time."
- Calling you when he/she knows you won't be at home to justify his/her obligation to remain in contact with you. ("Well, every time I call the claimant, he's not at home.")

In your dealings with the insurance company, always remember that you have paid the insurance company premiums for them to provide you with claims service. In actuality, you have paid the salary of the insurance company representative who is now avoiding you, and making your experience in claiming your rights a living nightmare.

Let's put it another way. Suppose you had just purchased a new washer from the local department store. They assured you that their service division would deliver the machine the next day. You wait around all day, no delivery. You call, leave messages and receive no returned calls.

It has now been two days and your new washer is nowhere in sight. Your blood is boiling, your temper is increasing, and you finally pick up the phone. You call the department store manager and give him an ear full, "I have paid for your merchandise and service. I demand efficient service, and if I don't get it, I'll climb your management ladder like a monkey in the zoo!" Whew! Talk about being assertive!

So ask yourself, why don't you demand service from your insurance company? Why do a large number of homeowners become intimidated by the delaying techniques used by adjusters? Why do some homeowners cower at the mere thought of dealing with the games adjusters play?

You can fight back by using common sense and creative communication.

Through the experience of others who have dealt with the unethical tactics of adjusters, we offer the following suggestions:

1. It cannot be overstated enough, ALL correspondence you send to the adjuster or claims office should be sent via certified mail, return receipt requested. This will prevent the unscrupulous adjuster from denying that they received your correspondence. Your return receipt will also indicate the date of delivery, which may prove important in contradicting an inaccurate statement by the adjuster.

2. If the adjuster fails to return calls on a regular basis, drop the adjuster a short note. In that note make certain that you specify an exact day and time in which you can be reached. Send a copy of this note to the claims office manager.

3. If the adjuster fails to make scheduled appointments at your home, go to his/her office and demand to talk to either the adjuster, the supervisor or manager. Stress the fact that you are now being inconvenienced and this is inappropriate conduct on the part of the adjuster.

4. Call the adjuster early in the morning or late in the day. Adjusters often get their assignments in the morning and upgrade their files in the afternoon. One aggressive claimant who had run out of patience, placed a call from a public telephone across the street from the insurance claims office. When told that the adjuster was out of the office and not accepting calls, the claimant walked across the street and entered the claims office. He found his delinquent adjuster shooting the breeze near the water cooler! Needless to say, the manager's office was the next stop.

THE INSURANCE COMPANY CHAIN OF COMMAND
(see chart on following page)

It is helpful for you to understand the chain of command that exists in the insurance company claims offices, as well as in the independent adjuster's claims office. The chain of command typically exists in this order:

• **Independent Adjusters:**

The independent adjuster does not have any authority to make coverage decisions. The independent adjuster can, of course, give his/her opinion as to coverage, but it is the company adjuster who hired the independent adjuster who makes that decision.

If you have a disagreement regarding the extent of damages with the independent adjuster, your next step would be to talk to the company adjuster and so on up the chain of command.

• **The Claims Adjuster (Field or Office):**

At the bottom of the chain of command is the claims adjuster. Your initial contact is usually with this type of adjuster. Claims adjusters have limited "official" power in claims matters. In any claims office, you will also have one or more senior adjusters. The senior claims adjuster can, and often does, offer claims advice to your personal claim adjuster, but is in no position to direct or enforce claims handling procedures for other adjusters. Some companies use the terms "staff adjuster" or "company adjuster" to describe the position of a claim representative who is directly employed by the insurance company. Claims adjusters are usually not required to be licensed.

• **The Branch Claims Supervisor:**

The next person up the chain of command is the supervisor. This individual is responsible for overseeing and directing the claims handling practices of a number of junior, office, field and/or senior adjusters within the office. If you cannot reach an agreement with the initial field or office adjuster assigned to handle your claim then you must ask to speak to the claims supervisor. This person can, and often does, overrule the decisions of the adjusters under him/her.

• **The Branch Claims Manager:**

The last person up the chain of command within the branch claims office is the claims manager, and your last appeal in any claims office. This person is responsible for overseeing every file that is being handled by every adjuster in the office. The claims manager has the authority to overrule the decisions of the claims supervisor. It is usually the claims manager who affixes his/her signature on denial letters that leave the office.

• **The Regional Manager:**

The regional manager oversees the operation of a designated number of branch claims managers within his/her given region. This manager normally deals with claims of value beyond the branch manager's authority. He or she also deals with claims that have entered a litigation or appraisal process, and will review and report to higher authorities on the course of action for these types of claims. The regional manager also will handle claims that are in dispute and cannot be resolved on the branch level. If you have exhausted all remedies available at the branch level, you should contact the regional manager and discuss your problem. Sometimes a simple call will bring results when the regional manager determines that additional assistance or raising the settlement offer will conclude the dispute and close the file. If you do not get a response or satisfactory resolve at this level, you can to on to the next person in the chain of command, the company vice-president.

• **The Insurance Company Vice-President:**

The vice-president is generally a public relations and operations coordinator. The vice-president controls and advises the day to day operations at the regional level. He or she is normally very cognizant of the public image of the company, and will intervene in a claim, no matter what value, especially if the dispute is creating a public relations nuisance or has the potential of "bad press."

TYPICAL INSURANCE COMPANY
CHAIN OF COMMAND
WITH AVERAGE AUTHORITY LIMITS*

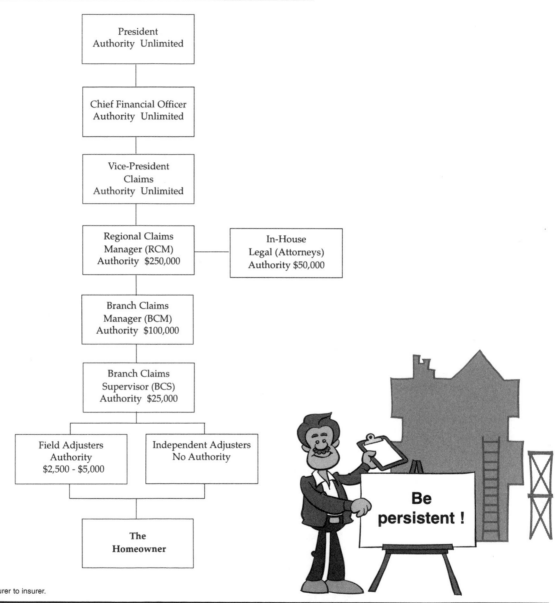

President
Authority Unlimited

Chief Financial Officer
Authority Unlimited

Vice-President
Claims
Authority Unlimited

Regional Claims
Manager (RCM)
Authority $250,000

In-House
Legal (Attorneys)
Authority $50,000

Branch Claims
Manager (BCM)
Authority $100,000

Branch Claims
Supervisor (BCS)
Authority $25,000

Field Adjusters
Authority
$2,500 - $5,000

Independent Adjusters
No Authority

The
Homeowner

Be persistent !

* Monetary authority may vary from insurer to insurer.

Note: One way to get calls through to difficult individuals is to make friends with the receptionist answering the claims office telephone. Being polite to that individual can be very rewarding. Receptionists have the undaunting task of coordinating all incoming calls. A sympathetic show of understanding to the difficulties of his/her job can work wonders. Ask his/her name (not in a demanding way, but as a new acquaintance). Then the next time you call the office, call the receptionist by name and, most likely, your call will be put through, whether or not the adjuster is trying to avoid you.

CHAPTER 11

BEEN DENIED - NOW WHAT?

- **DISSATISFIED?**

- **CONTACTING THE INSURANCE COMMISSIONER**

- **ALTERNATIVE REMEDIES - APPRAISAL, ARBITRATION, LAWSUIT**

- **FINDING AND SELECTING YOUR APPRAISER**

- **CAN I SUE FOR "BAD FAITH?"**

- **LEGAL COUNSEL**

DISSATISFIED?

If your dissatisfaction stems from the conduct or non-responsiveness of the adjuster assigned to your claim, review the sample letters contained in Chapter 15. These letters can be adapted to suit your needs and can be directed to specific individuals who are influencing your claim.

Some state insurance departments offer mediation services. In addition, most policies allow for an independent appraisal or arbitration process to resolve disputes over money. The decision of the appraiser(s) or the arbitrator is often binding. The decision, however, doesn't always close the door to mediation or litigation on other issues, such as "bad faith."

It is an important point to continually maintain your claim file. This file may prove invaluable if your claim is contested or if you bring forth an action of bad faith.

CONTACTING THE INSURANCE COMMISSIONER

Each state has an Insurance Commissioner. Most commissioners are appointed by the Governor of the state, although some are elected officials. The Insurance Commissioner's office is given the task of monitoring the activities of insurance companies, assuring proper compliance with state laws regulating insurance companies, and evaluating whether the insurance companies are solvent.

If you have any kind of question or problem regarding insurance in general, or a claim in particular, the Insurance Commissioner's office is available to offer you assistance. If you have a valid complaint against your insurance company, or you feel you are not being treated fairly, the Insurance Commissioner's office will investigate the issue. If there is a problem with your claim, the Insurance Commissioner's office can be a powerful force. Contact your own individual state's Department of Insurance and request to speak to someone on the staff of the Insurance Commissioner. (see Chapter 9 - "State Listings").

ALTERNATIVE REMEDIES -
APPRAISAL, ARBITRATION, LAWSUIT

Perhaps the most neglected section of any homeowner policy is the "Appraisal Clause." It can be found under the "Conditions" portion of any property insurance policy. It is such an important section of the policy for you, the policyholder, that it bears close scrutiny.

Following is a sample of the language you will find in most policies, especially the HO - 3 Homeowner Policy:

"If you and we fail to agree on the amount of loss, either one can demand that the amount of the loss be set by appraisal. If either makes a written demand for appraisal, each shall select a competent, independent appraiser and notify the other of the appraiser's identity within 20 days of receipt of the written demand. The two appraisers shall then select a competent, impartial umpire. If the two appraisers are unable to agree upon an umpire within 15 days, you or we can ask a judge of a court of record in the state where the residence premises is located to select an umpire. The appraisers shall then set the amount of the loss. If the appraisers submit a written report of an agreement to us, the amount agreed upon shall be the amount of the loss. If the appraisers fail to agree within a reasonable time, they shall submit their differences to the umpire. Written agreement signed by any two of these three shall set the amount of the loss. Each appraiser shall be paid by the party selecting that appraiser. Other expenses of the appraisal and the compensation of the umpire shall be paid equally by you and us."

The appraisal process is usually the most economical procedure to take rather than to immediately seek legal counsel. There is no guarantee that the appraisal will allow you to settle with the insurance company for the amount you feel is fair and reasonable for your damages. But, there is a good chance that you will at least settle far better than you would have if the appraisal process was not initiated at all.

If your policy contains an appraisal process clause, your insurance company might try to force you into the appraisal process. They may possibly send you an "official looking" letter saying you have 20 days or less to retain an appraiser. (This is a highly questionable ethical practice on their part). Do not be intimidated by this kind of pressure. A letter notifying you of your right to the appraisal process is not necessarily a demand by the insurance company to engage in one. You have the option to initiate the appraisal process but so does your carrier. The carrier will rarely initiate the appraisal process, but if they do, take note of the time for you to respond.

If you decide to enter the appraisal process and are dissatisfied with the outcome of the appraisal decision, you can sue your insurance company. Keep in mind if you elect to sue, that the <u>absence</u> of evidence of wrongdoing on the insurance company's representative(s) part during the appraisal process, will be vigorously defended by your insurance company and can be very expensive.

If there is not a mandatory arbitration clause in your policy, and your disagreement is based on the value of the claim, you can request arbitration (non-judicial) with your insurance company. If arbitration is agreed upon by both parties and your policy has an arbitration provision, then you both must agree as to whether the decision of the arbitrator will be binding or non-binding. If the parties decide that the arbitration will be binding, then the decision of the arbitrator will be final. If, however, the parties decide that the decision of the arbitrator will be non-binding, and you or your carrier receives an unsatisfactory result (or the insurance company will not agree to arbitration), you can elect to file a formal lawsuit and proceed to trial. Arbitration rules vary from state to state so it is a good idea to consult legal counsel when selecting this course of action.

After you file a lawsuit, a judge will review the case and determine the value of the claim. Next, based on the amount of the damages, the judge can determine whether the case may be arbitrated (judicial arbitration) or tried in a court of law.

If the judge sends the case to arbitration, the parties must agree as to whether the decision of the arbitrator will be binding or non-binding. (If an agreement cannot be reached, the decision will be non-binding). As in a non-judicial arbitration, a binding decision is final. If, however, the decision of the arbitrator will be non-binding, and you receive an unsatisfactory result, you can then request a "Trial de Novo," and the case will be put back into the trial court and either settled or tried. Arbitration is an alternative solution to a potentially costly trial.

Lawsuits are the absolute last resort if you have a dispute with your insurance company. Lawsuits are very expensive and demand a high level of commitment of your time and resources. They are often high-risk contests that usually don't compensate for the economic loss you will have suffered as a result of the money you will have invested in bringing the lawsuit. You may be justified in filing a formal lawsuit if you have suffered a major loss (and you have coverage under your policy) and your insurance company is continuing to deny your claim.

A final note: Your insurance company is obligated to notify you (after you have filed a claim) of an impending statute of limitations deadline. Generally, you have within one year from the date of loss to file a formal lawsuit. However, you should consult legal counsel or check with your state's Insurance Commissioner's office to determine the applicable statute of limitations, to ensure you are filing your lawsuit in a timely manner!

FINDING AND SELECTING YOUR APPRAISER

When you prepare to select an appraiser for your property damage dispute with the insurance company, remember that the word "appraiser" can mean a number of things. Generally, we refer to an appraiser as a kindly gent peering through an eyepiece to judge the value of your diamond-studded ring. If you browse through the yellow pages of your telephone directory you'll be amazed at how many appraisers offer this type of service. However, you are not looking for a jewelry appraiser if you need someone competent in the field of property damage claims.

The appraisal process requires an individual with skill and knowledge in the construction field. The appraiser should not just evaluate damage but have a thorough knowledge of the following:

• All facets of the construction trade
• Knowledge of engineering requirements
• Knowledge of material pricing
• Knowledge of material sources
• The labor and time elements related to repairs and reconstruction
• Speciality conditions and circumstances

The individual you choose as your appraiser will be required to represent you in the appraisal process through documentation and oral argument in front of the umpire assigned to hear the dispute.

Your appraiser must be:

• Articulate
• Persuasive (he or she will be conducting an argument on your behalf and in your best interest)
• Believable (he or she will have to convince the umpire that your position is right and the insurance company is wrong)
• A disinterested party (he or she should not have a financial connection to you, with the exception of the fee for his/her services. This also means that the appraiser cannot work for the company that will be doing the work on the damaged property or is in any way connected to the supplier of materials.)

If you have a problem finding a qualified property damage appraiser, you can hire an appraiser from the following fields for the purpose of representing you at the appraisal process:

• Attorneys (with knowledge of the construction trade)
• Architects
• Engineers
• A good restoration contractor who does not have a financial interest in the outcome of the appraisal.
• Remember again, any appraiser that you hire must not have a financial interest in the outcome of the appraisal process, with the exception of their normal fee for their services as an appraiser.

If you have a problem locating an appraiser, consider contacting a qualified restoration contractor, since they work with insurance companies on a daily basis. You may also, in addition to checking your local yellow pages, consider library sources, real estate brokers or mortgage offices. To determine a state approved appraiser, you can contact your state's Office of the Insurance Commissioner for assistance (see Chapter 9 - "State Listings").

One last thing to consider when interviewing your prospective choice for appraiser (talk to at least three prospects) is that you ascertain their "track record" and experience in their dealings with insurance carriers. Ask if they have ever been part of an appraisal process with your insurance carrier. Also determine what their history has been as far as the position they have taken in the past; for example, have they worked on behalf of the insurance company or on behalf of the homeowner claimant?

CAN I SUE FOR "BAD FAITH?"

Your insurance company is said to have a "fiduciary" relationship with its customers. This means the protection of the policyholder's property is held in trust by the insurance company, and therefore, the company owes the policyholder fair treatment. The insurance company is required to deal with you fairly and cannot take advantage of your lack of knowledge or deprive you of claim payments you are entitled to as an insured.

When an insurance company violates the fiduciary relationship with its customer and neglects to provide the protection called for by the policy, the company may be seen as acting in "bad faith."

In order for bad faith to exist, there usually must be conscious wrongdoing on the part of the insurance company and not merely an honest mistake.

In order to determine if your claim warrants a bad faith action you usually have to meet a number of requirements. It should be noted that bad faith actions are unique to their own circumstances and evidence, and the following list should not be an indication or suggestion that this is all you are required to prove in order to file a bad faith claim, or to be successful in the outcome. Items to consider include, but are not limited to:

- Determining coverage at the time of loss and were you covered by the applicable policy?
- Does your insurance contract subject the insured to damages over and above whatever may be due under the contract?
- Has the insurance company failed to perform its implied duties under the contract?
- Has the insurance company committed fraud, negligent misrepresentation, intentional infliction of emotional distress, etc.?
- Are punitive damages applicable?
- Has the insurance company withheld benefits, denied benefits due, paid less than due, or unreasonably delayed payment?

Because the insurance company's officers, agents and representatives are not a party to the insurance contract, you usually cannot sue them individually. You are suing your insurance company directly on the basis of the conduct or "unreasonable practices" of the company's representatives.

The following conduct by an insurance company has been held admissible to show it acted "unreasonably":

- Failure to investigate claim thoroughly
- Failure to evaluate claim objectively
- Unduly restrictive interpretation of claim form
- Using improper standards to deny claim
- Dilatory claims handling
- Deceptive practices to avoid payment of claim
- Abusive or coercive practices to avoid payment of claim
- Disregard for the insured's rights
- Unreasonably low settlement offers
- Unreasonable litigation or litigation tactics to avoid payment of claim

In most jurisdictions, if you sign a release with the insurance company you may waive your rights to pursue an action of bad faith against your insurance company.

Please note that in order to undertake a lawsuit for bad faith, you should consult legal counsel because of the complexities and legal theories that are required to bring such an action.

LEGAL COUNSEL

The use of lawyers often is an economic decision. If you have followed the recommendations contained in this book, you will have laid the groundwork in an organized fashion for the lawyer to take over. This should provide you with a great deal of savings of both money and time.

Lawsuits are an action of last resort. You can win, or at least get the amount you think you're owed, but it could take years, especially since insurers may certainly appeal any verdicts against them. It doesn't make sense to file suit if you're going to end up paying a lawyer more than the amount of your claim.

In some limited cases, there may be a provision in your insurance policy allowing the prevailing party to recover their attorney fees.

CHAPTER 12
GETTING PAID
BY THE INSURANCE COMPANY

- **PARTIAL PAYMENTS - ADVANCES**

- **YOUR MORTGAGE COMPANY IS ON THE CHECK**

- **TAXES AND THE INTERNAL REVENUE SERVICE**

PARTIAL PAYMENTS-ADVANCES

Partial payments and advances are not an obligation of your insurance company. The practice of advance payment is an industry standard, but is not necessarily a service your insurance company must provide.

Most insurance companies will advance payment for living expenses and emergency repairs before you are able to obtain receipts.

Remember that any advance payment or partial payment will be deducted from your final settlement.

YOUR MORTGAGE COMPANY IS ON THE CHECK

Most homeowners have a mortgage on their home. All of the standard homeowners policies contain a mortgage clause that requires the insurance company to name the mortgage holder on payment drafts. The reason for the clause is simply to protect the mortgagee's interest in the property.

An individual or firm holding a mortgage on a piece of property has a vested interest in seeing that the property is secure and kept in good repair.

BEFORE ENDORSING AND CASHING ANY CHECKS FROM YOUR INSURANCE COMPANY, LOOK FOR ANY LANGUAGE ON THE CHECK THAT MAY BE CONSIDERED A RELEASE LIMITING YOU FROM FURTHER ACTION.

When a mortgage company is named as a payee on a settlement draft or check, problems can arise because the mortgage company can choose to hold on to all of the funds until the repairs are completed. This can be hard on you, especially if you are dealing with a contractor who is not financially solvent enough to complete the work before getting paid.

Also, it is essential that you keep your mortgage payments up to date. If you don't, it may give the mortgage company justification either to call your loan in or to take the proceeds of the settlement and apply them toward your mortgage. If the amount of your rebuilding settlement is greater than the amount of your mortgage, the mortgage company should release the difference to you. The mortgage company generally has no legal basis for holding more than you owe.

Keep in mind that if you have hired a top quality restoration contractor to do your loss rebuild or repair, he/she will generally complete the work before expecting payment from the insurance company for their services. This takes the financial load off of you, and you can most likely rest assured that you are dealing with a solvent company who can perform your work request immediately.

If you are dealing with other types of repair persons, the mortgage company may only advance approximately 10% of the monies held to commence the work. The rest of the payments throughout the job will be distributed in progress payments as work is completed. Usually, the mortgage company will require inspections to be performed to verify that the work has indeed been done.

Some states have laws that require mortgage companies to deposit insurance settlements into interest-bearing accounts. But in states that lack such a law, contact your mortgage company and suggest alternatives to release the money that may be withheld. If necessary, you can contact an attorney for assistance.

TAXES AND THE INTERNAL REVENUE SERVICE

An insurance claim filed by you may be something you should consider on your tax return. As a taxpayer, you may be allowed to "write off" certain losses. These losses might include those not covered by insurance, or portions of losses that are not covered.

The law generally does not allow deductions for losses that would be covered by insurance but were not claimed.

If the insurance company does not pay the full value of the loss, you may be able to deduct the difference between what you received from the insurance company and the value of the loss (as a tax write-off). In many cases, the amount you paid for your insurance deductible is a tax deduction as well.

You should consult your accountant or tax preparer for information and advice on deducting insurance losses.

CHAPTER 13
HIRING THE "RIGHT" CONTRACTOR(S)

- **YOU, THE HOMEOWNER, ACTING AS THE OWNER-BUILDER/ GENERAL CONTRACTOR**

- **THE RESTORATION CONTRACTOR**

- **THE GENERAL CONTRACTOR**

- **THE SPECIALTY CONTRACTOR**

- **THE HANDYMAN**

- **CHECKING OUT THE PROSPECTIVE CONTRACTOR**

- **ABOUT ARCHITECTS AND ENGINEERS**

The key here is hiring the "right" contractor. This means going beyond hiring a contractor that is licensed and has all of his/her insurances, but one that is fully qualified for your particular restoration. Fully qualified means either being able to perform the work to a respected level of knowledge and quality in the industry, or has the employees or subcontractors capable of doing so.

Always remember the saying "jack of all trades and master of none" and beware; we all know what happened to the house that Jack built!

REMEMBER, THE CHOICE OF CONTRACTOR IS YOURS TO MAKE !!!

As a general rule:

- There is nothing in your homeowners policy that says you must use the contractor recommended by your insurance company.
- There is no requirement that you obtain at least three bids prior to submitting your claim.
- There is no requirement that you pick the lowest bid available.

Rebuilding or repairing your home is a very personal project. Considering this and the amount of money you will be spending, you deserve personal and professional service. You should hire only qualified licensed contractors!

Although most contractors are responsible, hardworking professionals, some are not. Horror stories of jobs gone wrong are not unusual.

Finding a contractor who is right for you can be difficult. Unless you have already used a contractor you are happy with, your search will require time and investigation. Be aware that after a serious loss event such as a firestorm or earthquake, contractors move into the area from other parts of the country or "would-be" contractors try to cash in. **Do not rush into repairs or rebuilding. Take time to consider all your alternatives!**

YOU, THE HOMEOWNER, AS THE OWNER-BUILDER / GENERAL CONTRACTOR

Many homeowners will attempt to assume the role of a general contractor after experiencing an insurance loss. The problem with this is that the homeowner usually is not knowledgeable in the many tasks a general contractor must perform.

Obtaining building permits, on-site official inspections, etc., can be mind-boggling to an individual not trained and experienced in this endeavor.

Also, when a homeowner takes on the responsibility as general contractor, he/she must also assume all liability associated with the work. This means worker's compensation insurance, high priced building materials, public liability exposure and unforeseen pitfalls.

A homeowner, assuming the role of general contractor, cannot include in the insurance claim a demand for 10% overhead allowance and 10% profit because they are not entitled to "profit" from their loss.

THE RESTORATION CONTRACTOR

The restoration contractor that specializes in insurance restoration work is the most versatile of all the contractor categories you can choose. Restoration contractors provide immediate emergency services, such as window board up, roof repair, mop up and cleaning and/or structural support engineering, just to name a few. The restoration contractor generally, if not always, has the background of a general contractor but also specializes in the knowledge of insurance claims and the processing and handling of those claims from submission to negotiation of settlement. Unlike the other types of contractors, emergency service restoration contractors work <u>with</u> the insurance companies, as well as <u>for</u> the homeowners. Their knowledge and skills in writing an accurate scope of repairs is instrumental in obtaining an expeditious and complete settlement.

Another valuable consideration in hiring a restoration contractor is his/her experience in the sequencing and scheduling of other tradespeople involved in the repair or rebuild of your home. Restoration contractors, unlike other types of contractors, spend a great deal of time working with others you will need in order to return your home to its original condition.

A good insurance restoration contractor that has insurance expertise has the ability to handle and process claims faster because of the experience he/she has had with the insurance companies in the past.

Restoration contractors know the correct and most efficient way to write a scope of repairs. They know how to write supplemental claims and know the techniques required to deal with all types of insurance adjusters.

Building and replacement materials can be obtained at better costs, and the quality of work is supreme, since their main interest is repair and rebuild, rather than new home construction. Restoration contractors should also procure all required building permits and other official documents needed for the repair or rebuild of your home and he/she should be familiar with all regulatory codes. Restoration contractors should be licensed, bonded, and insured which offers you the protection and security of knowing your insurance claim dollars will be put to good use and quality workmanship.

THE GENERAL CONTRACTOR

The general contractor is primarily involved with the construction of new homes, alterations or room additions.

General contractors are exceptional in their respective fields, but their knowledge of insurance claims and claims processing is often limited.

THE SPECIALTY CONTRACTOR

The specialty contractor is just what the name implies. They have a specialty. For example, the specialty contractor may be an expert in drywall construction or they may be a house painter. His/her "specialty" limits their ability to subcontract other repair people because they do not carry out this task on a regular basis. Specialty contractors may low-bid on a particular job, only to find themselves in a quandary attempting to schedule and sequence the work to be done by subcontractors. Their expertise lies in their particular "specialty," and generally not in efficiently operating a repair team, which a good restoration contractor does on a regular basis.

THE HANDYMAN

Diametrically opposed to the restoration contractor is the handyman. Using a handyman to repair and rebuild is akin to using a medical student to perform bypass surgery. Handymen do have a place in the construction business, but their role should be limited to simple repairs and appliance installation. Handymen are normally uninsured and unlicensed.

In California, for example, under the Contractor's License Law, a licensed contractor utilizing an unlicensed handyman for work done in excess of $300 (including labor and materials), jeopardizes the contractor's license and he/she can be subjected to a fine of $10,000!

CHECKING OUT THE PROSPECTIVE CONTRACTOR

Once you have located a prospective contractor, you will want to begin by interviewing him/her. In regard to interviewing, above all else, ask questions! The more questions you ask, the more you reduce your risk of being disappointed later. First, you will need to establish the contractor's basic credibility. To do so, tactfully obtain the following information:

1. Is the contractor licensed?

All valid contractors are licensed by the State Contractors Licensing Board. To determine if the contractor you are considering is licensed, ask to see his/her contractor's pocket license and some additional form of identification. The names on the license and the other identification should corre-

spond. It is illegal for one contractor to use another contractor's license. As an added precautionary measure, you should call the Contractors State License Board to confirm that the license is valid. Generally, a contractor who has a lower license number has been in business longer than a contractor with a higher number.

2. Is the contractor a member of a local professional organization?

You should contact the contractor's local professional or trade association to see if the contractor you are considering is a member and, if so, one of good repute. These associations often provide a means of settling disputes, if and when they arise. For future reference, you may want to determine if the association in your area offers this service.

3. Does the contractor have worker's compensation and liability insurance coverage?

If the contractor does not have coverage for injury to his workers on the job and for others that may be injured during construction, you may be held responsible as the property owner. The liability insurance would also protect against property damage. Be sure that you are named as an additional insured on the contractor's general liability, worker's compensation or other insurance policies. Insurance companies can provide evidence of coverage by issuing a Certificate of Insurance to you outlining the contractor's insurance coverage. This certificate will advise you of the limits of liability, the name of the insurance company, the coverage provided and the effective dates of the policies. The insurance company will usually provide you notice in case of policy cancellation. It is preferable that the contractor be covered by an insurance company that is licensed by your state's Department of Insurance.

4. **Is the contractor bonded?**

In California, all licensed contractors are required to post $7,500 either in cash or in a bond with a surety company when a license is issued.

This bond is known as the Contractor's License Bond. The bond does not necessarily guarantee performance. The bond amount is very small and is payable to all legitimate claimants who can prove that a violation of certain provisions of the Business and Professions Code was in fact committed by the contractor. This can be very difficult to prove and should not be relied upon by consumers for protection.

5. **How long has the contractor been in business?**

6. **What type of buildings does the contractor construct or repair (residential, commercial, etc.)?**

7. **Where are the buildings located (so that you can inspect them)?**

8. **Does the contractor have references or previous customers that you can call?**

Skilled contractors are proud of their work and will be happy to give you references. At a minimum, the contractor should be able to give you a list of the addresses of recently repaired or rebuilt houses, subdivisions, town-houses or condominium complexes. Look at homes that are the same style as your house.

9. **Check other material suppliers.**

You may want to ask the contractor for references from material suppliers, subcontractors and financial institutions to determine whether the contractor is financially responsible. Ask the suppliers about the contractor's payment history or if any lien processes have been used against this contractor.

10. **Does the contractor work in the field himself/herself or does he/she perform construction management?**

Depending upon the company, either method may work well. For many people, however, a more hands-on arrangement is reassuring.

ABOUT ARCHITECTS AND ENGINEERS

If a complete or partial rebuild of your property is necessary, an architect's services and those of an engineer, may be required to draw up plans and other specifications.

If you indeed require an architect, his/her plans are essential to estimate bids for labor and materials. An architect may not be needed unless you have suffered a major loss, such as your home was completely destroyed by fire.

You may also have the need to employ an engineer. There are a variety of engineers to choose from to satisfy your needs in damage assessment or reconstruction. The reports and evaluations of these experts can also be used as evidence in potential legal actions should the need arise.

Soils Engineer

Generally, a registered civil engineer with the title "soils engineer" or "geotechnical engineer" has been granted the title by the Board of Registration for Professional Engineers and Land Surveyors. A soils/geotechnical engineer has specialized knowledge, training, and experience in the sciences and mathematics related to analyzing foundations, earth pressures, slopes, embankments, seepage, drainage, pavements, containments, and related aspects of engineering geology.

The soils engineer has two main tasks: (1) to identify geologic or geotechnical hazards that might pose a threat to construction, such as landsliding or creep, erosion, expansive soils, faulting, and settlement; and (2) to develop an engineered solution, often in conjunction with the structural engineer, to mitigate such hazards, for example, through the use of retaining walls and proper selection of foundation types.

The soils engineer generally works very closely with the structural engineer, civil engineer, architect, and building contractor. While the earth-moving phase of construction is occurring, the soils engineer will visit the site to examine cutaways and evaluate the soils for proper compaction.

- *Do not let payments get ahead of the work completed.*

- *ALWAYS . . . ALWAYS . . . ALWAYS get unconditional lien releases from <u>everyone</u> who has supplied materials or labor to your property before you pay them!*

Structural Engineer

Generally, structural engineers are registered separately by the Board of Registration of Professional Engineers and Land Surveyors. A structural engineer has specialized knowledge, training, and experience in the sciences pertaining to the analysis and design of force-resisting systems for structures such as foundations and retaining walls.

Typically, structural engineers do not play a substantial role with conventional residential construction since residential building codes are fairly standardized. However, there are circumstances in which a structural engineer should be consulted. These include unusual or difficult site conditions such as hillsides, ravines, or where unstable earth is present. In these instances, the structural engineer would recommend structural solutions to mitigate those problems.

With regard to commercial buildings, structural engineers do play a significant role in advising the architect and contractor of pertinent structural design requirements.

For a structure which has been damaged as a result of natural forces (earthquake, wind, flood, fire, etc.), consultation with a structural engineer is recommended to determine if the surviving structural components are sufficient to support reconstruction of the original building.

Be sure when you are choosing an architect or engineer that you ask him/her questions concerning their experience, training, and formal schooling.

Also, make inquires into the architect's or engineer's last project and the party who hired them to do the work. Ask the questions: What kind of projects, similar to yours, have they done? What is their workload? Are they willing to commit to a schedule? Will they oversee the progress of the work? Can they give you references?

Tactfully ask about, and independently verify, their insurance coverage, called "Errors and Omissions" (E & O) insurance. This type of insurance coverage will protect you if a mistake in drawing and planning (or other services offered by these professionals) is negligently made.

All architects and engineers should be licensed and you should verify their license through your state's Department of Consumer Affairs.

CHAPTER 14

STARTING THE RESTORATIONS

- **BUILDING DEPARTMENT REQUIREMENTS**

- **ON-SITE MEETING WITH BUILDING INSPECTORS**

- **SCHEDULING THE WORK - ROUND TABLE MEETINGS**

- **ITEMS YOU SHOULD CONSIDER IN THE CONSTRUCTION AGREEMENT**

- **ADDITIONAL WORK ORDER**

- **CHANGE ORDER**

- **SUPPLEMENTAL CLAIMS**

- **WHAT ARE PRELIMINARY LIEN NOTICES AND MECHANIC'S LIENS?**

- **LIEN WAIVERS AND RELEASES (Conditional and Unconditional)**

BUILDING DEPARTMENT REQUIREMENTS

Whenever any type of rebuild or repair is done on a residential dwelling, the local government's permit and inspection departments become factors.

The purpose of the building department requirements is to provide minimum standards to safeguard life or limb, health, property and public welfare. The building department regulates and controls the design, construction, quality of materials, use and occupancy, location and maintenance of all buildings and structures within a given jurisdiction.

Procuring building permits and scheduling inspection dates is completely unknown territory to most homeowners. Remember that building department requirements vary from state to state and city to city.

Unless you were instrumental in the design and construction of your home, and have experienced the myriad of bureaucratic paperwork involved in obtaining the necessary permits and licenses, be prepared to take on city hall without the use of a road map.

In general, the Uniform Building Code™ provides the necessary requirements prior to starting construction or reconstruction efforts.

*Under the Uniform Building Code™, Section 106, sub-section 106.1, entitled "Permits Required," it states, in part: "....no building or structure regulated by this code shall be erected, constructed, enlarged, altered, repaired, moved, improved, removed, converted or demolished unless a separate permit for each building or structure has first been obtained from the building official."

Your own state or county's regulations may vary, but the Uniform Building Code™ is a model which many states, counties, cities and towns have adopted.

Your own state, county or municipality's building codes may also list those structures of work areas that are exempt from the requirements of obtaining a permit.

Some examples of exemptions may include the following:

- One-story detached accessory buildings used as tool and storage sheds, playhouses and similar uses, provided the projected roof area does not exceed 120 square feet.

- Fences not over 6 feet.

- Oil derricks.

- Movable cases, counters and partitions not over 5 feet 9 inches tall.

- Retaining walls which are not over 4 feet in height measured from the bottom of the footing to the top of the wall, unless supporting a surcharge or impounding Class I, II or III-A liquids.

- Water tanks supported directly upon grade if the capacity does not exceed 5,000 gallons and the ratio of height to diameter or width does not exceed 2 to 1.

- Platforms, walks and driveways not more than 30 inches above grade and not over any basement or story below.

- Painting, papering and similar finish work.

- Temporary motion picture, television and theater stage sets and scenery.

- Window awnings supported by an exterior wall of Group R, Division 3 Occupancy and Group M Occupancies when projecting not more than 54 inches.

- Prefabricated swimming pools accessories to a Group R, Division 3 Occupancy in which the pool

walls are entirely above the adjacent grade and if the capacity does not exceed 5,000 gallons.

Obtaining a Permit

To obtain a permit, the applicant shall first file an application, in writing, on a form furnished by the code enforcement agency for that purpose. Applications generally require the following:

1. Identify and describe the work to be covered by the permit for which application is made.

2. Describe the land on which the proposed work is to be done by legal description, street address or similar description that will readily identify and definitely locate the proposed building or work.

3. Indicate the use or occupancy for which the proposed work is intended.

4. Be accompanied by plans, diagrams, computations and specifications and other data, as required.

5. State the valuation of any new building or structure or any addition, remodeling or alteration to an existing building.

6. Be signed by the applicant or the applicant's authorized agent.

ON-SITE MEETING WITH BUILDING INSPECTORS

*The Uniform Building Code™ Section 108, entitled "Inspectors," requires that,..."all construction or work for which a permit is required shall be subject to inspection by the building official and all such construction or work shall remain accessible and exposed for inspection purposes until approved by the building official."

All permits issued to the permit holder or agent of the permit holder shall have to post, or otherwise make available, an Inspection Record Card.

This is to allow the inspection official to conveniently make required entries regarding the progress and completion of the work.

It is the responsibility of the homeowner (if one assumes the role of general contractor) or the party doing the work to notify the building official that the work is ready for inspection.

The building official may require at least a one day notice prior to inspection. This notice may be in writing or by telephone, depending on the policy of that particular building official. At the time of the scheduled inspection, complete access to the work area must be provided.

Work cannot proceed on a particular portion of a required permit until it has successfully been approved by the building official.

SCHEDULING THE WORK-ROUND TABLE MEETINGS

If you elect to supervise the restoration of your property and assume the role of general contractor, you will be inheriting all the responsibility, woes and worries associated with that position.

One of the first things that you must organize is a "round table meeting" of all the tradespeople required for your work project.

After you have contacted all the tradespeople needed to effectuate a rebuild of your home following your loss, you must then meet with these professionals to coordinate the commencement, progress, and completion of the work. Not only is this a scheduling challenge, you must also "talk the talk, and walk the walk." In other words, you'd better be cognizant of the language of the industry.

Let's use the example of an insurance loss that encompasses the rebuild of one room.

You have aligned all the tradespeople needed: a plumber, an electrician, a carpenter and a roofer.

Next, you need to determine who will do what first. You must be available to monitor the repair work as it

progresses and be prepared for the possibility of absences at the work site or other unforeseen delays which might conflict with the next phase of the project.

Scheduling work roles is a tremendous undertaking, unless you have had prior experience at general contracting. This is where the services of a qualified restoration contractor can make these worries, frustrations and anxieties all go away.

The restoration contractor, more than likely, has a working relationship with the type of tradespeople that you have selected. The restoration contractor has the experience in dealing with subcontractors and sequencing the work events as they happen.

Also, the restoration contractor knows what to look for in the inspection and assessment of a work project. They monitor the progress of the job, which is the quality control aspect of job performance and work progression.

The restoration contractor should be knowledgeable of all building permits and regulation codes required. The restoration contractor can also find suitable substitutes for material and components that may be delayed in shipping or deliverance, to assure that the work continues without disruption or delay (see Restoration Schedule on the following page).

ITEMS YOU SHOULD CONSIDER IN THE CONSTRUCTION AGREEMENT

The following will give you a brief explanation of the structure, terms and pitfalls to avoid in preparing and signing an agreement with a contractor.

An important thing to remember is: Do not sign any legal agreement if you do not understand, or agree with, all of the terms and conditions of that agreement. If you are unsure of what you will be signing, contact an attorney who is knowledgeable in handling this type of agreement. Also, since no situation is exactly the same, the terms and conditions of any agreement may vary.

All agreements must state the parties to the agreement. This should be concise and clear to all parties involved. Individuals doing business as a company name must enter into agreements individually, and cannot use just the company name.

RESTORATION SCHEDULE

START DATE _2_, _3_, _00_   WEEK _/_ OF _/_   PAGE _/_ OF _/_

WORK DESCRIPTION	MON	TUE	WED	THU	FRI	SAT	SUN
GET ROOF PERMIT	x AM						
TEAR OFF EXISTING ROOF AND HAUL AWAY DEBRIS		x AM					
HAVE ROOF SHEATHING INSPECTED			x AM				
INSTALL NEW ROOF			x				
CALL FOR FINAL ROOF INSPECTION					x		
SCRAPE AND REPAIR CEILING			x				
SPRAY ACOUSTICAL CEILING MATERIAL ON CEILING							x
PAINT INTERIOR						x	
CLEAN CARPETS						x	
x = starting date							

All agreements must be definite and clear. Any ambiguity or indefiniteness in the terms and conditions of the agreement is to be construed against the author of the agreement.

All agreements must exchange what the law refers to as "consideration." For example, you are exchanging money, and your contractor is exchanging services for that money. The financial terms of the agreement must be explicitly clear.

All agreements must have a starting date and a completion date for performance. There should also be a clause in the agreement to cover the eventuality of late work performance and the penalty for such lateness.

All agreements should have remedial clauses. In other words, know your options should the contract not be fulfilled. For example, can you have the matter arbitrated or must you immediately proceed to court for a judgment?

All agreements must be dated and signed by both parties. Keep a completed and signed copy for yourself.

Never sign a blank or partially prepared agreement. If an agreement has space on the paper between the last term or condition and the signature block, draw lines or scribble "x's" in the vacant area as to prevent anyone from making additional entries after you sign.

If you and your contractor have discussed added work, substitutions of materials or equipment, or changes in the completion date, make sure that clearly worded and signed "change orders" reflect this.

In some states, when you enter into certain types of agreements with a contractor, you have three business days to review the contract to ensure that it meets your satisfaction. In other states, however, you may have 72 hours. Check your own state's law regarding the time period for the right of rescission. You should be able to make changes within this period, with the mutual consent of your contractor, or you might even be able to cancel the contract during this time period. Remember to put all changes in writing, and if you decide to cancel the contract, notify your contractor in writing of your desire to cancel.

Be sure your agreement describes the materials to be used. The quality, quantity, color, weight, size and brand name are very important. This information is normally contained in the contractor's work order, which is an integral part of your agreement. Never enter into an agreement without a clear description of the materials and the labor required to accommodate your project.

Any warranties that the contractor or manufacturer offers should also be in writing and attached to the agreement by way of reference.

Be sure to verify the other party's signature and company affiliation before signing the agreement. The signature block should include full name, address, license number and company title, if applicable.

ADDITIONAL WORK ORDER

An additional work order is for services provided by the contractor which were not included in the original agreement.

CHANGE ORDER

A change order is a written authorization provided by the homeowner to the contractor approving a change from the original plans, specifications or other contract documents, as well as a change in the cost. With proper signatures, a change-order is considered a legal document. It is a good practice to get all change orders in writing.

SUPPLEMENTAL CLAIMS

Supplemental claims deal with items of loss (hidden damage) discovered after the initial scope of repairs has been submitted.

The initial inspection will reveal damage of immediate noticeable concern, while undetected damage may lie internally in the structure or interior of your home (i.e., in walls, ceilings, floors, etc.). Newly discovered damage will necessitate a supplemental claim.

Insurance adjusters are aware of the possibilities of such claims, and usually will consider these types of post submitted claims as due course in the final settlement. However, if a supplemental claim is presented in an untimely manner (way beyond the initial claims submission), close scrutiny of the discovery of such damage will delay and possibly cause denial of that portion of your claim. In any case, do not sign a release until all issues are resolved.

WHAT ARE PRELIMINARY LIEN NOTICES & MECHANIC'S LIENS?

Generally, most states have laws that provide for those who furnish labor or materials to your home. Labor and/or material suppliers can record a "Claim of Lien" or "Mechanic's Lien" against your home if they are not paid, even if you paid your contractor in full in accordance with your contract with him/her. If your contractor fails to pay the labor or material suppliers who performed work or supplied materials in connection with your project, a lien can be placed against your home!

If you don't get unconditional lien releases from all the labor and material suppliers, you could be required to pay the same bill twice to keep from losing your home.

In California, the state law requires that before entering into a contract, contractors must give you the following notice:

NOTICE TO OWNER

> "Under the California Mechanic's Lien Law, any contractor, subcontractor, laborer, supplier, or other person or entity who helps to improve your property, but is not paid for his or her work or supplies has a right to place a lien on your home, land, or property where the work was performed and to sue you in court to obtain payment.

> This means that after a court hearing, your home, land, and property could be sold by a court officer and the proceeds of the sale used to satisfy what you owe. This can happen even if you have paid your contractor in full if the contractor's subcontractors, laborers, or suppliers remain unpaid.

> To preserve their rights to file a claim or lien against your property, certain claimants such as subcontractors or material suppliers are each required to provide you with a document called a "Preliminary Notice." Contractors and laborers

who contract with owners directly do not have to provide such notice since you are aware of their existence as an owner. A preliminary notice is not a lien against your property. Its purpose is to notify you of persons or entities that may have a right to file a lien against your property if they are not paid. In order to perfect their lien rights, a contractor, subcontractor, supplier, or laborer must file a mechanic's lien with the county recorder which then becomes a recorded lien against your property. Generally, the maximum time allowed for filing a mechanic's lien against your property is 90 days after substantial completion of your project."

TO HELP ENSURE EXTRA PROTECTION FOR YOURSELF AND YOUR PROPERTY, YOU MAY WISH TO TAKE ONE OR MORE OF THE FOLLOWING STEPS:

1. Require that your contractor supply you with a payment and performance bond (not a license bond), which provides that the bonding company will either complete the project or pay damages up to the amount of the bond. This payment and performance bond, as well as a copy of the construction contract, should be filed with the county recorder for your further protection. The payment and performance bond will usually cost from 1 to 5 percent or more of the contract amount depending on the contractor's bonding ability. If a contractor cannot obtain such bonding, it may indicate his/her financial instability.

2. On larger projects, require that payments be made directly to subcontractors and material suppliers through a joint control. A joint control company is a licensed escrow company that specializes in handling funds for construction jobs. Funding services may be available in your area, for a fee, which will establish voucher or other means of payment to your contractor. These funding services may also provide you with lien waivers and other forms of protection. Any joint control agreement should include an "Addendum to Control Agreement Escrow Instructions." This addendum must be signed by you, your contractor, and a representative of the joint control company.

3. Issue joint checks for payment, made out to your contractor and subcontractors or material suppliers involved in the project. The joint checks should be made payable to the persons or entities which send preliminary notices to you. Those persons or enti-

ties have indicated that they are claiming lien rights on your property, therefore, you need to protect yourself. Issuing joint checks will help to ensure that all persons due payment are actually paid.

4. Upon making payment on any completed phase of the project, and before making any further payments, require your contractor to provide you with unconditional "Waiver and Release" forms signed by all material suppliers, subcontractors, and laborers involved in that portion of the work for which payment was made. The statutory lien releases are set forth in exact language in Section 3262 of the California Civil Code. Many stationery stores sell a version of the "Waiver and Release" forms if your contractor does not have them. The material suppliers, subcontractors and laborers that you obtain releases from are those persons or entities who have served preliminary notices to you. If you are not certain of the material suppliers, subcontractors, and laborers working on your project, you may obtain a list from your contractor. On projects involving improvements to a single-family residence or duplex owned by individuals, the person(s) signing these releases loses the right to file a claim against your property. In other types of construction, this protection may still be important, but may not be as complete.

To protect yourself under this option, you must be certain that all material suppliers, subcontractors, and laborers have signed the "Waiver and Release" form. If a mechanic's lien has been recorded against your property, it can only be voluntarily released by a recorded "Release of Mechanic's Lien," signed by the person or entity that recorded it. However, a mechanic's lien will be ineffective unless a lawsuit to enforce it is filed in a timely manner. You should not make any final payments until any and all such liens are removed and all unconditional lien releases have been obtained. You should consult an attorney if a lien is filed against your property.

LIEN WAIVERS & RELEASES
(Conditional and Unconditional)

DO NOT MAKE ANY PAYMENTS UNLESS YOU GET LIEN RELEASES!

• Conditional Waiver and Release Upon Progress Payment

The conditional waiver and release upon progress payment form is used when your payment to the claimant(s) (contractor/subcontractors, material suppliers, etc.) has been paid up to date for the work which has already been done. However, a conditional lien release does not release you from a subcontractor or supplier who is not paid!

For your protection, issue joint checks to all labor and material suppliers your contractor has used once you have received a current lien release.

• Unconditional Waiver and Release Upon Progress Payment

Many banks require an unconditional waiver and release form upon progress payment before clearing an additional draw on construction loans. This form is used to assure the homeowner and bank that all contractors, subcontractors and all other parties that have provided material, labor and services, have been paid to date and that no rights to claims exists.

All parties (contractor, subcontractors, material suppliers, etc.) signing this form waive their rights - whether paid or not - to pursue an action against you. The Unconditional Waiver specifies that the party (by way of his/her signature) affirms that all work to date has been paid in full to date. Make sure that all parties that have provided labor, material supplies and services sign this document. Get a release from <u>everyone</u> before you pay them!

• Unconditional Waiver and Release Upon Final Payment

The unconditional waiver and release upon final payment form is used as the final waiver and release for work performed by contractors, subcontractors, material suppliers, etc. When your restoration project is complete, have all material suppliers, subcontractors, their laborers and anyone else that provided service to your project, complete and sign this form <u>before</u> you give them the final payment!

When the parties providing the above services affix their signature to the unconditional waiver, they waive all rights to file a Mechanic's Lien against you and your property to recover payment due for any money owed to them for performance of the job.

IN CHAPTER 16 OF THIS BOOK, THERE ARE LIEN WAIVERS & RELEASES FOR YOU TO USE. IN ALL CASES, BEFORE USING THESE FORMS, CHECK WITH YOUR OWN STATE'S LAWS AND REQUIREMENTS.

THE "SMALL LITTLE DETAILS" (SLD) LIST

The Small Little Details list (see form in Chapter 16) is an innovative concept that gives the homeowner control of the progress and corrections to be made during the rebuild project.

At the "nearing completion phase" of your project, small little details could be a concern. These may include painted areas that have been missed, flooring that has not been completely restored, mislocated electrical outlets, inoperable ceiling fans and so on.

Utilizing the SLD form provided in Chapter 16 of this book, the homeowner can monitor the quality control of the work project on a daily basis. Entries can be made as the work progresses.

A copy of the Small Little Details form should be presented to the contractor for his or her review and confirmation. If the contractor agrees to correct the details on your list, be sure to get his/her signature on the SLD form. The original form will be your permanent record of notification to your contractor of the corrections in construction which must be resolved and should be corrected before receiving final payment from you.

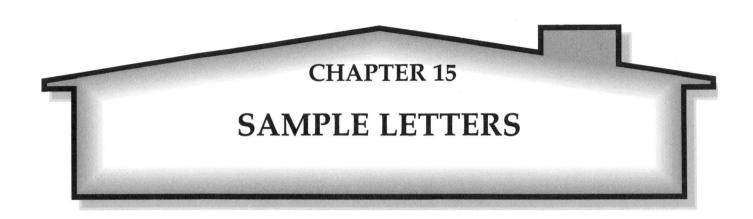

CHAPTER 15

SAMPLE LETTERS

The following are samples of letters that you, the homeowner, might use when communicating with insurance companies. Each letter is identified by a title and has an explanation for different situations.

Draft of Notice of Claim (Notification of Loss)

Draft of Submission of Claim Package

Draft of Letter Due to an Adjuster Being Non-Responsive

Draft of Letter to be Sent Through the Insurance Company "Chain of Command"

Draft of Letter of Dissatisfaction

Draft of an Appraisal Letter

DRAFT OF NOTICE OF CLAIM (Notification of Loss)

Situation: Notification to your insurance carrier of your property loss. At this point it is not necessary to assess the cause of the damage, since you may have not yet had the opportunity to ascertain the actual cause of damage. ALL IMPORTANT LETTERS SHOULD BE SENT VIA CERTIFIED MAIL, RETURN RECEIPT REQUESTED!

Date:

To: (Your Insurance Company)
        AnyStreet
        Anytown, USA

Attention: Claims

Re: Notification of New Claim

Dear Gentleperson:

This notice of claim letter is intended to serve as notification of my recent loss under policy number _____. This notice satisfies the requirement contained in the "Conditions-Claimant Responsibility to Notify" section of my insurance policy.

The damage to my property occurred on _____, 19__ , at approximately _____(AM/PM).

I have not yet compiled a complete inventory of my loss, but will prepare any documents needed to expedite my claim and settle this matter as needed or required under my policy conditions.

I understand that my claim will be receiving a claim number and assigned to a claims adjuster to facilitate the processing of my claim. I would like to be notified as soon as possible as to the claim number and the adjuster assigned to my claim. I also request the adjuster's direct telephone number and fax number in order that I may work directly with him/her to resolve my claim swiftly and equitably.

Please send any documents needed, such as a "Proof of Loss" form, at your earliest convenience. Likewise, I shall provide an estimate of damages for your evaluation and will be submitting an entire claims package to your adjuster's attention in the very near future.

If there are any questions, your adjuster can contact me at (___) 123-4567.

Thank you, in advance, for your cooperation in this matter.

Very truly yours,

DRAFT OF SUBMISSION OF CLAIM PACKAGE

Situation: You are about to submit your claim to the insurance company. **ALWAYS SEND COPIES OF YOUR DOCUMENTS AND ESTIMATES OF DAMAGE.** *Be completely prepared in sending documentation of your loss. Make sure your estimate of repair (scope of repairs - see Chapter 8) is well-prepared, photographs or videos being sent are copies and not originals, and all other pertinent documentation are NOT ORIGINALS. Be sure to send this letter with your documentation by certified mail, return receipt requested in order to obtain a verification of the acceptance by the insurance company. If you hand deliver your "claims package," insist that the person accepting on behalf of the company gives you a receipt for the delivery of your package.* **Note:** *The items mentioned in the sample letter below may or may not be items you may be submitting. Usually the Proof of Loss form (see Chapters 5 and 16) is submitted prior to the submission of damage documentation once it has been requested by the assigned adjuster, but a copy of the Proof of Loss form can be sent with the claims package as well.* **ALL IMPORTANT LETTERS SHOULD BE SENT VIA CERTIFIED MAIL, RETURN RECEIPT REQUESTED!**

Date:

To: (Your Insurance Company)
AnyStreet
Anytown, USA

Attention: [Mr./Ms.]_____(Your assigned adjuster's name)

Re: Your Insured: [Your Name]
Claim Number: [Your assigned claim number]
Policy Number: [Your policy number]
Date of Loss: [The date the loss occurred]

Dear [Mr./Ms.]_____: (Your assigned adjuster's name)

Pursuant to my insurance coverage and conditions contained in my policy as noted above, I submit the enclosed claim documentation for payment. I include in this package my Proof of Loss form, my scope of repairs, photographs taken immediately after the loss and copies of expenses I incurred concerning the emergency services needed.

I am aware that you may need a couple of days to evaluate the materials I have enclosed, so I will diary a date ten (10) days from the date of this letter/package and contact you on that date. If you have any questions, please do not hesitate to contact me at (___) 123-4567.

I look forward to a swift and mutually equitable resolution of this claim.

Very truly yours,

DRAFT OF LETTER DUE TO AN ADJUSTER BEING NON-RESPONSIVE

Situation: You have had extreme difficulty getting your assigned adjuster to respond to your calls and letters. You feel your claim has been put "on hold" while the adjuster is unavailable. This has delayed your claim too long, and you want to take preliminary action to notify the adjuster of his/her non-responsiveness. You should send a copy of this letter to the assigned adjuster's supervisor by way of a "cc" attachment. This is not to create animosity or to get the adjuster into trouble, but is intended as a precaution against misdirected mail or misfiling. ALL IMPORTANT LETTERS SHOULD BE SENT VIA CERTIFIED MAIL, RETURN RECEIPT REQUESTED!

Date:

To: (Your Insurance Company)
          AnyStreet
          Anytown, USA

Attention: [Mr./Ms.]_____(Your assigned adjuster's name)

Re: Your Insured: [Your Name]
          Claim Number: [Your assigned claim number]
          Policy Number: [Your policy number]
          Date of Loss: [The date the loss occurred]

Dear [Mr./Ms.]_____: (Your assigned adjuster's name)

        The notice of my claim was initially submitted to your office on ___ ___ ___. Since that time, I have experienced extreme difficulty in contacting you. I have left numerous messages and even sent a letter on _____ indicating my displeasure at how my claim has been handled. I also have been informed of your company's obligation under the Unfair Claims Settlement Practices Act that you must promptly resolve claims and avoid unnecessary delay.

        I have fulfilled my obligations under our insurance contract and have met the requirements of my policy provisions and conditions, but I am increasingly perplexed over your lack of responsiveness regarding this claim. The delay of this claim has been unreasonable and I have not been given a proper explanation. I would like to see this matter concluded to our mutual benefit.

        If I do not hear from you or your supervisor within ten (10) days from the date of this letter, I will assume that I should seek someone of higher authority within your office or choose an alternative option.

                      Very truly yours,

cc: (Your assigned adjuster's supervisor)

DRAFT OF LETTER TO BE SENT THROUGH THE INSURANCE COMPANY "CHAIN OF COMMAND"

*Situation: Your attempt to get a response from your assigned adjuster is falling on deaf ears. You may have a valid argument concerning your estimate for damages versus the estimate by the insurance company's adjuster. You wish to make a request for a change in adjusters and you also feel that the non-responsive adjuster is not very experienced in the area of your particular claim damage. You may have to take a step up the "Chain of Command" to reach someone who will take another look at your claim and the evidence of your loss. (You should take the appropriate steps to reach the branch claims office level - see Chapter 10). This letter should be addressed to the adjuster's supervisor. **After that, if you still don't get adequate satisfaction from your request, send a copy of this letter with a cover letter to the branch claims manager and, if need be, to the vice-president of the company.** Simply ask the office receptionist for the name, telephone number and mailing address of your assigned adjuster's supervisor. <u>ALL IMPORTANT LETTERS SHOULD BE SENT VIA CERTIFIED MAIL, RETURN RECEIPT REQUESTED!</u>*

Date:

To: (Your Insurance Company)
         AnyStreet
         Anytown, USA

Attention: [Mr/Ms.]. _____, Supervisor (Your assigned adjuster's supervisor)

Re: Your Insured: [Your Name]
         Claim Number: [Your assigned claim number]
         Policy Number: [Your policy number]
         Date of Loss: [The date the loss occurred]

Dear [Mr./Ms.]_____: (Your assigned adjuster's supervisor)

I understand you are the supervisor of the assigned adjuster to my claim, [Mr.\Ms.]_____. I have had difficulty in communicating with this adjuster and feel that [his/her] assessment of my claim has been undervalued, and also that [he/she] lacks the essential construction knowledge to properly evaluate any reasonable settlement. [He/she] has remained inflexible regarding the compromise of my claim and has indicated by [his/her] inflexibility that there is virtually nothing more to talk about. I do not desire to deal with this person anymore regarding the processing of my claim, and I formally request that another adjuster be assigned to this matter.

I am taking appropriate steps to inform you of my dissatisfaction in the way my claim has been handled. I assume that you, as a supervisor, oversee the conduct of your adjusters and that you are the appropriate person to whom my concerns should be addressed. If you lack the authority to honor my requests, please notify me and I shall seek redress elsewhere.

I do expect a response from you no later than ten (10) days from the date of this letter to avoid having to forward this matter to your branch claims manager.

                         Very truly yours,

DRAFT OF LETTER OF DISSATISFACTION

Situation: Your claim for damages and all the appropriate documentation has been submitted to the assigned adjuster. He/she has offered an amount to settle your claim which you feel is entirely unreasonable and unrealistic. You are not making the choice of replacing the adjuster, but you do want someone with more experience to view your claim file and reconsider the settlement offer. This letter of dissatisfaction can be non-adversarial in nature and even may increase your settlement amount while maintaining a good relationship with your insurance company. ALL IMPORTANT LETTERS SHOULD BE SENT VIA CERTIFIED MAIL, RETURN RECEIPT REQUESTED!

Date:

To: (Your Insurance Company)
AnyStreet
Anytown, USA

Attention: [Mr / Ms.]. _____, (Your assigned adjuster's supervisor)

Re: Your Insured: [Your Name]
Claim Number: [Your assigned claim number]
Policy Number: [Your policy number]
Date of Loss: [The date the loss occurred]

Dear [Mr./Ms.]_____: (Your assigned adjuster's supervisor)

I wish to bring to your attention a matter involving your adjuster assigned to handle my claim, [Mr./Ms.]_____.

On [month, day, year], [Mr./Ms.]_____(the assigned adjuster) presented me with an offer to settle my claim in the amount of $_____. Based on the amount of damages that I have sustained, this offer is totally inadequate and unacceptable. [Mr./Ms.]_____ (the assigned adjuster) has appeared to have been responsive in [his/her] dealings regarding my claim, with the exception of the assessment of the total value of the claim.

I am requesting that you as [Mr./Ms.]_____(the assigned adjuster)'s supervisor, review my claim file and reconsider my settlement demand previously voiced to your adjuster. I feel that with a fresh look at the file and damages incurred, along with the combination of your expertise and knowledge of the claims process, we will be able to come to a mutually acceptable and equitable resolution to this matter.

Since I have been a long time insured of your company, I am also sending a copy of this letter to my agent in order to keep [him/her] apprised of the status of this claim file.

I await your immediate reply.

Very truly yours,

cc: (Your insurance agent)

DRAFT OF AN APPRAISAL LETTER *(See Chapter 11 Before Considering Using This Letter!)*

*Situation: This letter can be used by the insured homeowner as a demand for the appraisal process should he/she face a situation in which the company and the insured have come to an impasse in negotiations and a neutral party must be brought in to settle the matter. When liability is agreed upon but the amount of damages is in dispute, wherein both sides cannot agree upon a mutually acceptable amount, they may utilize the appraisal process clause of most insurance policies. The appraisal process is normally initiated by the insured (claimant) and rarely chosen as a remedy by the insurer. When a demand for the appraisal process is given, you and the other side may only have a certain number of days (usually 20 days, or the amount of time dictated by your policy) to prepare for the appraisal process. BE SURE YOU HAVE RETAINED A CONSTRUCTION APPRAISER, WITH FULL KNOWLEDGE OF THE PROCESS, BEFORE DEMANDING AN APPRAISAL PROCESS UNDER THE PROVISIONS OF YOUR POLICY. Remember, the clock starts ticking the moment your insurance company receives notice of your demand for the appraisal process. Also keep in mind that the time limit requirements may vary from state to state. **AN APPRAISAL DEMAND SHOULD BE ADDRESSED TO THE BRANCH CLAIMS MANAGER.** ALL IMPORTANT LETTERS SHOULD BE SENT VIA CERTIFIED MAIL, RETURN RECEIPT REQUESTED!*

Date:

To: (Your Insurance Company)
       AnyStreet
       Anytown, USA

Attention: [Mr/Ms.]. _____, (the name of the branch claims manager)

Re: Your Insured: [Your Name]
       Claim Number: [Your assigned claim number]
       Policy Number: [Your policy number]
       Date of Loss: [The date the loss occurred]

Dear [Mr./Ms.]_____ : (the name of the branch claims manager)

This appraisal letter is to notify _____ (name of your insurance company) that I hereby demand appraisal of my damages as specified in my homeowners policy, Section_____, under the Conditions provision where the appraisal process clause appears.

My claim was submitted in accordance with the requirements of the policy and I accommodated every request for documentation of my claim made by the assigned adjuster [Mr./Ms.]_____.
When it came time to settle this matter, I was presented with an offer made by your representative which was undervalued, unrealistic and unacceptable. The adjuster displayed inflexibility and refused to reconsider my counteroffer to settle this matter. I addressed a letter to the assigned adjuster's immediate supervisor on (month/day/year) and did not get a satisfactory response or solution to the dispute. A copy of the prior letter was also sent directly to you on (month/day/year). (see situation box in the "Chain of Command" letter.)

Having exhausted all informal efforts to resolve this matter, except the final appraisal process afforded to me under the appraisal clause in my insurance policy, I now wish to exercise the rights to which I am entitled. I have already selected a competent and disinterested appraiser who will make an appraisal of the damages to my _____(name the area of damage, such as; roof, walls, ceilings, etc.) and submit his/her findings to your appraiser and, subsequently, to their mutually selected umpire. According to my homeowners policy, you have [_____days] from the receipt of this official demand for appraisal within which to select your own competent and disinterested appraiser. Advise me of the name of your appraiser and where he/she can be reached. I will then forward this information to my appraiser. The returned certified mail receipt has verified that proper notice has been given to your company of my demand for the appraisal process. I would appreciate a follow-up letter or telephone call indicating receipt of this notice, and if your company has changed positions concerning this issue.

       Very truly yours,

CHAPTER 16
FORMS TO USE AND MODIFY
DEPENDING ON THE NATURE OF YOUR CLAIM

Loss Summary

Telephone/FAX Log

Fax Transmittal Sheet

Claims Processing Information Checklist

Expense Log

Damage /Photo List

Photo Page

Chronology of Events

Sworn Statement in Proof of Loss

10-Point Claims Submission Checklist

Scope of Repairs

Contractor Questionnaire

Restoration Schedule

Restoration Agreement

Work Order

Supplemental Claim

Additional/Change
Work Authorization

Conditional Waiver and Release
Upon Progress Payment

Unconditional Waiver and Release
Upon Progress Payment

Unconditional Waiver and Release
Upon Final Payment

Restoration "Small Little Details" (SLD) List

Be as accurate as possible in your documentation, but also know, that in the event of a lawsuit, any information in writing may be obtained in a court of law as evidence.

LOSS SUMMARY
PERSONAL NOTES

For your personal reference, with respect to your loss, give a brief description of who was present, what happened, when it happened, where it happened, how it happened and why it happened. If it was a weather-related loss, note the weather conditions, and the direction the storm was coming from. Also note TV/ radio stations that made announcements regarding the storm. It is also a good practice to save newspaper clippings regarding the storm.

NOTE: Do not list calls to your attorney in order to maintain the right to your attorney-client privilege.

B OF: _____

DATE	TIME	RESPONSE

FAX TRANSMITTAL SHEET

If you have received this communication in error, please notify us immediately by telephone at the phone number below. Telephone costs will be reimbursed. Thank You!

❑ **FAX ONLY**   ❑ **VIA FAX AND MAIL**   ❑ **VIA FAX AND CERTIFIED MAIL**

TO:

COMPANY:

FAX:

DATE:

FROM:

PHONE:

FAX

TOTAL PAGE(S) INCLUDING COVER

❑ PLEASE CALL ASAP	❑ ACKNOWLEDGE RECEIPT	❑ ATTACHMENTS
❑ PLEASE RETURN ASAP	❑ MATERIAL AS REQUESTED	❑ PICTURES
❑ PLEASE PROCESS ASAP	❑ NO ACTION REQUIRED	❑ PROOF OF LOSS
❑ PLEASE CALL FOR MEETING TIME	❑ FOR YOUR RECORDS	❑ SCOPE OF REPAIRS
❑ PLEASE COMPLETE AS INDICATED	❑ _____	❑ NOTICE OF COMPLETION

MESSAGE REGARDING CLAIM NO: _____

CLAIMS PROCESSING INFORMATION CHECKLIST

1. Determine Your Assigned Adjuster's Name _____ ❑

2. Determine Claim Number _____ ❑

3. Telephone Number of Office _____ ❑

4. Office FAX number _____ ❑

5. Adjuster's Direct Telephone Number _____ ❑

6. Mailing Address of Office _____ ❑
   _____

7. Supervisor's Name _____ ❑

8. Claims Manager's Name _____ ❑

9. Home Office Telephone Number _____ ❑
   (If you can't obtain from branch
   office, request it from agent.)

10. Name of Person Who Claim was Reported to: _____ ❑

11. Date and Time Claim Was Reported: _____ ❑

EXPENSE LOG

DATE: _____

CLAIM NO. _____

PAGE _____ OF _____

JOB NAME: _____

_____

ADDRESS: _____

_____

CITY: _____

_____

	Date	Paid to	Description	Amount	Total
1					
2					
3					
4					
5					
6					
7					
8					
9					
10					
11					
12					
13					
14					
15					
16					
17					
18					
19					
20					
21					
22					
23					
24					
25					
26					

TOTAL

DAMAGE / PHOTO LIST

JOB OF:

ITEM	PHOTO #	DESCRIPTION

PHOTO PAGE

CLAIM #_____

INSURED_____

PAGE_____OF _____

↗

PHOTO # _____
BRIEF DESCRIPTION: _____

_____

_____

_____

↗

PHOTO # _____
BRIEF DESCRIPTION: _____

_____

CHRONOLOGY OF EVENTS

JOB OF: ....

DATE	TIME	DESCRIPTION

SWORN STATEMENT IN PROOF OF LOSS

Insured:_____ Insured by:_____

Address:_____ Policy Number:_____

City:_____ Date issued:_____ Date exp:_____

State:_____ Zip:_____ Agent:_____

Hm. Tel._____ Agency:_____

Wk. Tel. _____ Tel. Number:_____

Physical Address of Insured Property:_____

To:_____
        Insurance Company

At time of loss you insured the above physical property against loss as described under Schedule "A" according to the terms and conditions of the above indicated policy of insurance and all forms, endorsements, transfers and assignments attached thereto.

1.   Time and Origin: A _____ loss occurred about the hour of _____o'clock _____M.,on the _____day of _____19____. The cause and origin of said loss were: _____
_____
_____

2.   Occupancy: The building described, or containing the property described, was occupied at the time of loss as follows, and for no other purpose whatsoever: _____

3.   Title and Interest: At the time of the loss the interest of your insured in the property described therein was: _____ No other person or persons had any interest or incumbrance thereon, except: _____.

4.   Changes: Since the said policy was issued there has been no assignment thereof, or change of interest, use, occupancy, possession, location or exposure of the property described, except: _____
_____

5.   Total Insurance: The total amount of insurance upon the property described by this policy was, at the time of the loss, $_____, as more particularly specified in the apportionment attached under Schedule "C", besides which there was no policy or other contract of insurance, written or oral, valid or invalid.

6.   The Actual Cash Value of said property at time of loss was.   .   .   .   .   .$_____

7.   The Whole Loss and Damage was.   .   .   .   .$_____

8.   Less Amount of Deductible   .   .   .   .$_____

9.   The Amount Claimed under the above numbered policy is   .   .   .   .   .$_____

The said loss did not originate by any act, design or procurement on the part of your insured, or this affiant; nothing has been done by or with the privity or consent of your insured or this affiant, to violate the conditions of the policy, or render it void; no articles are mentioned herein or in annexed schedules but such as were destroyed or damaged at the time of said loss; no property save has in any manner been made. Any other information that may be required will be furnished and considered a part of this proof.

FOR YOUR PROTECTION CALIFORNIA LAW REQUIRES THE FOLLOWING TO APPEAR ON THIS FORM:
Any person who knowingly presents a false or fraudulent claim, for the payment of a loss, is guilty of a crime and may be subject to fines and confinement in state prison.

State of _____   _____

County of_____

                                                _____
                                                Insured Date

Subscribed and sworn to before me this_____day of _____19_____

_____Witness

10-Point Claims Submission Checklist

1. Photograph/Video of damaged areas or components ❏
   (Remember: When you have your film processed,
   request double prints so you can retain one copy.)

2. Summary of the Loss ❏
   (A short description of the loss, including the date,
   time, the cause of the loss and if there were any
   witnesses.)

3. Claim Submission Cover Letter ❏
   (Addressed to the proper party and be sure
   to reference, at the top of the letter, the claim number
   and date of loss.)

4. Sworn Statement Proof of Loss Form ❏
   (This is your sworn statement that a loss occurred.)

5. Scope of Repair Report ❏
   (Be sure to retain the original report.)

6. Damaged Inventory List ❏
   (This "list" should pertain to home content losses.)

7. Claim Assignment ❏
   (If you have assigned your claim to a restoration contractor.)

8. All Documents Sent are Copies ❏

9. Properly Addressed Package ❏
   (Mail your "claim package" directly to your assigned
   adjuster. Make sure of postage to avoid return and delay.)

10. Mail Via Certified Mail ❏
    (Return receipt requested)

136

SCOPE OF REPAIRS

INSURED _____   INSURANCE CO. _____

ADDRESS _____   POLICY # _____

CITY STATE ZIP _____   CLAIM # _____

H/PH _____   DATE OF LOSS _____

B/PH _____   TYPE OF LOSS _____

AREA NAME _____   AREA DIMENSIONS _____   PG____OF____

DESCRIPTION	#/U	U/M	PPU	COST

SCOPE OF REPAIRS

INSURED _____

ADDRESS _____

CITY STATE ZIP _____

H/PH _____

B/PH _____

INSURANCE CO. _____

POLICY # _____

CLAIM # _____

DATE OF LOSS _____

TYPE OF LOSS _____

AREA NAME _____ AREA DIMENSIONS _____ PG____OF____

DESCRIPTION	#/U	U/M	PPU	COST

LEGEND							
AMP-Amperes	CFDAY-Cost/CF/Day	EST-Estimated Amount	LF-Lineal Feet	PR-Pair	SFF-Sq Foot of Floor	SYF-Sq Yd Floor	U/M-Unit of Measure
AVG-Average	CY-Cubic Yards	H-Height	LI-Lineal Inch	R&R-Remove/Replace/Reset	SFW-Sq Foot of Walls	SYL-Sq Yd Linoleum	V-Volts
BINS-No. of Bins	D-Depth	HRS-No. of Hours	L/M-Labor& Materials	S/C-Service Charge	SQ-Square of Roofing	SYW-Sq Yd Walls	W-Wide
CF-Cubic Feet	Days-No. of Days	L-Long	M/C-Minimum Charge	SF-Square Feet	SY-Square Yard	T&G-Tongue & Groove	w/-With
	EA-Each Unit	LDS-No. of Loads	PPU-Price per Unit	SFC-Sq Foot Ceiling	SYC-Sq Yd Ceiling	TK/D-Truck Loads per Day	#/U-No. of Units

SCOPE OF REPAIRS

INSURED _____

ADDRESS _____

CITY STATE ZIP _____

H/PH _____

B/PH _____

INSURANCE CO. _____

POLICY # _____

CLAIM # _____

DATE OF LOSS _____

TYPE OF LOSS _____

AREA NAME _____   AREA DIMENSIONS _____   PG____OF____

DESCRIPTION	#/U	U/M	PPU	COST

LEGEND	CFDAY-Cost/CF/Day	EST-Estimated Amount	LF-Lineal Feet	PR-Pair	SFF-Sq Foot of Floor	SYF-Sq Yd Floor	U/M-Unit of Measure
AMP-Amperes	CY-Cubic Yards	H-Height	LI-Lineal Inch	R&R-Remove/Replace/Reset	SFW-Sq Foot of Walls	SYL-Sq Yd Linoleum	V-Volts
AVG-Average	D-Depth	HRS-No. of Hours	L/M-Labor& Materials	S/C-Service Charge	SQ-Square of Roofing	SYW-Sq Yd Walls	W-Wide
BINS-No. of Bins	Days-No. of Days	L-Long	M/C-Minimum Charge	SF-Square Feet	SY-Square Yard	T&G-Tongue & Groove	w/-With
CF-Cubic Feet	EA-Each Unit	LDS-No. of Loads	PPU-Price per Unit	SFC-Sq Foot Ceiling	SYC-Sq Yd Ceiling	TK/D-Truck Loads per Day	#/U-No. of Units

Contractor Questionnaire

Type of Contractor: ❏ Handyman ❏ Specialty ❏ General ❏ Restoration

Business Name_____ License No._____ Exp._____

Address_____

City_____ St_____ Zip_____

(1) Tel No._____ (2) Tel No._____

Pager No._____ Fax No._____

Areas of Expertise_____,_____,_____,_____

Owner's Name_____ Home Phone_____

Address_____

City_____ St_____ Zip_____

Contractor License No._____ Expiration Date_____ Years in Business_____

Workers Compensation Insurance Carrier _____

Policy No._____ Expiration Date_____

Any claims_____ If yes, explain _____

General Liability Insurance Carrier _____

Policy No._____ Expiration Date_____

Any Claims_____ If yes, explain _____

SUPPLIER CREDIT REFERENCES

1. Name_____ Address_____

   City_____ St_____ Zip_____ Tel._____

2. Name_____ Address_____

   City_____ St_____ Zip_____ Tel._____

3. Name_____ Address_____

   City_____ St_____ Zip_____ Tel._____

Questions to ask suppliers:

1. How long has the contractor been doing business with you?

2. What does the contractor purchase from you?

3. How does the contractor pay for materials?

4. Does the contractor take discounts?

5. Has the contractor ever made late payments?

140

JOB REFERENCES - 3 MOST RECENT JOBS

1. Name_____ Address_____
   City_____ St_____ Zip_____ Tel._____
2. Name_____ Address_____
   City_____ St_____ Zip_____ Tel._____
3. Name_____ Address_____
   City_____ St_____ Zip_____ Tel._____

Questions to ask job references:

1. How long has the contractor been doing business with you?

2. What did the contractor do for you?

3. How did the contractor pay for materials?

4. Did the contractor ask for large draws?

5. Did the suppliers send you preliminary lien notices?

6. Did the contractor do everything as stated?

7. Did the contractor keep your property clean while the job was in progress?

8. Did the contractor have high standards of workmanship?

9. Did the contractor's employees and subcontractors respect you and your property?

10. Did the contractor provide you with unconditional lien releases from all suppliers and everyone that worked on your job?

11. Would you use the contractor again on a more expensive project that required a lot of fine detail?

Comments:

_____
_____
_____
_____
_____
_____
_____
_____

RESTORATION SCHEDULE

START DATE ____ / ____ / ____   WEEK ____ OF ____   PAGE ____ OF ____

WORK DESCRIPTION	MON	TUE	WED	THU	FRI	SAT	SUN

This is a sample of a general agreement with some provisions you may want
to consider as different states and situations may vary.

Restoration Agreement

RECITALS

1. _____, a specialty subcontractor (hereinafter called "Contractor"), agrees to provide the following labor, materials and construction in accordance with plans and specifications as may be added and initialed by the parties and attached hereto:

Contractor's Name:_____

Address:_____

Telephone:_____

City:_____State:_____

Contractor's License Number:_____

Owner (Buyer)_____

Address:_____

City:_____State:_____

TERMS AND CONDITIONS

2.   The work to be performed under this agreement shall be described in the individual work orders and change orders, which are hereby made a part of this agreement by this reference.

3.   The project ("Job") will be constructed according to drawings and specifications that have been examined by Owner and that have been or may be signed by the parties to this contract, unless otherwise specifically provided in the drawings or specifications. Contractor will obtain and pay for all required building permits and Owner will pay assessments and charges required by public bodies and utilities for financing or repaying the cost of sewers, storm drains, water service, and other utilities including sewer and storm drain reimbursement charges, revolving fund charges, hookup charges and the like.

4.   Any subsequent amendment, modification or agreement which operates to alter this contract, and which is signed or initialed by Contractor and Owner, shall be deemed a part of this contract and shall be controlling in case of conflict, to the extent that it alters this contract.

5.   If Owner, Construction Lender, or any public body or inspector directs any modification or addition to the work covered by this contract, the amount for such extra work shall be determined in advance and the cost shall be added to the contract price, plus contractors, usual fee for overhead and profit. Payments for extra work will be made as the extra work progresses, concurrently with payment made under payments scheduled. Contractor shall do no extra work without the prior written authorization of the Owner. Any such authorization shall show the agreed terms and shall be approved by both parties.

6.   All material removed from structures in course of alteration shall be disposed of by Contractor except those items designated by Owner in writing prior to commencement of construction. All Contractor's construction debris is to be removed by Contractor at termination of work and premises left in neat, broom-clean condition, unless otherwise agreed upon herein.

7.   Contractor agrees to start and diligently pursue work through to completion, but shall not be responsible for delays for any of the following reasons: failure of the issuance of all necessary building permits within a reasonable length of time, funding of loans, disbursement of funds into funding control or escrow, acts of neglect or omission of Owner or Owner's employees or Owner's agent, acts of God, stormy or inclement weather, strikes, lockouts, boycotts, or other labor union activities, extra work ordered by Owner, acts of public enemy, riots or civil commotion, inability to secure material through regular recognized channels, imposition of Government priority or allocation of materials, failure of Owner to make payments when due, or delays caused by inspection or changes ordered by the inspectors of authorized government bodies, or for acts of independent contractors, or holidays, or other causes beyond Contractor's control.

8.   Contractor will carry Worker's Compensation Insurance to protect Contractor's employees during the progress of the work. Owner shall obtain and pay for insurance against injury to his own employees and persons under Owner's direction and persons on the job site at Owner's invitation.

9.   Contractor guarantees that all materials furnished by him will be of standard quality free from defects, and will be installed or applied in a good and workmanlike manner. Such labor and materials are guaranteed for a period of one (1) year when subject to normal use and care, and provided Owner has complied in full with terms and payments and other conditions of this contract. The liability of the Contractor for defective material or installation under this guarantee is hereby limited to the replacement or correction of said defective material and/or installation, and no other claims or demands whatsoever shall be made upon or required to be allowed by the Contractor.

However, equipment, assemblies or units purchased by Contractor included in this contract are sold and installed subject to the manufacturer's or processor's guarantees or warranties, and not Contractor's.

10.	Owner agrees to sign and record a Notice of Completion within five (5) days after the project is completed and ready for occupancy. If Owner fails to so record the Notice of Completion, then Owner hereby appoints Contractor as Owner's agent to sign and record a Notice of Completion on Owner's behalf. This agency is irrevocable and is an agency coupled with an interest. Contractor may bar occupancy of the project by Owner or anyone else until Contractor has received all payments due under this contract and until Notice of Completion has been recorded. Use and/or occupancy shall be considered completion.

11.	If a funding control service is utilized, then Contractor and Owner hereby agree that the funding control service shall be appointed as Owner's agent to sign and record a Notice of Completion on Owner's behalf.

12.	Any notice required or permitted under this contract may be given by ordinary mail at the address contained in this contract, but such address may be changed by written notice from one party to the other from time to time. Notice shall be considered received one (1) day after depositing in the mail, postage prepaid.

13.	This contract, including documents incorporated herein by reference, constitutes the entire agreement of the parties. No other agreements, oral or written, pertaining to the work to be performed under this contract exists between the parties.

14.	This agreement shall be construed in accordance with, and governed by, the laws of the State of _____.

15.	If corrective or repair work of a minor nature remains to be accomplished by Contractor after the project is ready for occupancy, Contractor shall perform the work expeditiously.

16.	If major items of corrective or repair work remain to be accomplished after the building is ready for occupancy, the cost of which aggregates more than one percent (1%) of the gross contract price, the Owner pending completion of the work, may withhold payment of a sufficient amount to pay for completion of the work, but shall not withhold any greater amount.

17.	Contractor agrees to be bound by the following conditions when performing Job:

	a)	Contractor shall perform Job between the hours of 8:00 a.m. and 5:00 p.m.

	b)	At the end of each day's work, Contractor's equipment shall be stored at the premises described herein as Job site. All equipment must be stored in a safe area and any injury or potential or real liability to any person(s) or property as a result of such end of day storage, shall be construed and implied against Contractor.

	c)	At the end of each day's work, Contractor agrees to clean all debris from the work area and leave all appliances and facilities in good working order.

	d)	Contractor agrees that disruptively loud activities shall be performed only between 8:00 a.m. and 5:00 p.m.

	e)	Contractor agrees to confine all work related activity, materials and products, including dust and debris, to the areas described as work to be performed herein contained in this agreement.

	f)	All state and local permits necessary for performing services shall be paid by Homeowner and obtained before work begins by Contractor.

18.	Job shall be considered completed upon approval by Homeowner, provided that Homeowner's approval shall not be unreasonably withheld. Substantial performance of Job in a workmanlike manner shall be considered sufficient grounds for Contractor to require payment by Homeowner.

19.	If Contractor's performance is late, Contractor agrees that Homeowner shall be damaged in the amount of_____dollars ($_____) per day, and that Contractor shall be liable for such sums, which may be credited against any sums owed to Contractor by Homeowner.

20.	If Contractor, or any of his employees, helpers, agents, and subcontractors are injured in the course of performing Job, Homeowner shall be exempt from liability for such injuries to the extent allowed by law.

21.	Contractor agrees to indemnify Homeowner for all liabilities to third parties, known and unknown, which may arise from the performance of work and to obtain adequate business liability insurance that will cover Job.

22.	If any dispute arises under the terms of this agreement, the parties agree that the dispute shall be decided by the applicable small claims court if the amount in dispute is within the court's jurisdiction, and otherwise by binding arbitration under the rules issued by the American Arbitration Association. The decision of the arbitrator shall be final.

23.	Reasonable attorneys' fees of the prevailing party shall be paid by the other party.

24.	Any provisions in this agreement found to be invalid shall have no effect on the validity of the remaining provisions.

25.	All agreements between the parties related to Job are incorporated in this contract. Any modifications to the contract shall be in writing.

26.	Additional Terms or Conditions:

_____

_____

_____

_____

THIS DOCUMENT CONSISTING OF THIS AGREEMENT, PLANS, SPECIFICATIONS WORK ORDERS, CHANGE ORDERS, ADDITIONAL WORK ORDERS AND "NOTICE TO OWNER" (WHEN APPLICABLE), ALL ATTACHED HERETO AND MADE A PART HEREOF, SHALL CONSTITUTE THE AGREEMENT.

This agreement is executed by Homeowner and Contractor at:_____**on**_____

Owner's Signature _____

Contractor's Signature_____

Work Order

Page_____ of _____

NO:

SUBCONTRACTOR INFORMATION	JOBSITE INFORMATION
To:	Address:
Address:	City: State: Zip:
City: State: Zip:	Job Contact:
Tel	(W) Tel: (H) Tel:

SPECIAL INSTRUCTIONS

❑ Work Hours: _____ To _____
❑ Call Property Owner/Tenant If Going To Be Late
❑ Call Property Owner Upon Job Arrival.

❑ Call Job Contact Before Arrival
❑ Do Not Work Weekends
❑ Call Property Owner With Daily Progress

❑ Do Not Disturb Owner/Tenant
❑ Owner/Tenant Works Nights
❑ Call Property Owner Upon Completion

DESCRIPTION OF WORK TO BE PERFORMED:

•ALL WORK TO INCLUDE PROTECTION OF ALL PERSONAL AND REAL PROPERTY AND TO HAVE DAILY MINIMUM BROOM FINISH CLEANUP AND DEBRIS REMOVAL•

PAYMENT FOR ABOVE WORK IS: _____ *Dollars* $ _____

TERMS: _____

ABOVE WORK TO BE PERFORMED AS SPECIFIED FOR THE ABOVE PRICE UNLESS OTHERWISE STIPULATED IN WRITING PRIOR TO JOB START.

WE HEREBY AGREE TO FURNISH LABOR AND MATERIALS COMPLETE IN ACCORDANCE WITH THE ABOVE SPECIFICATIONS UNDER THE TERMS AND CONDITIONS OF OUR AGREEMENT, AT THE ABOVE STATED PRICE.

Property Owner: _____ Date: _____

Subcontractor Signature _____ Date: _____

SUPPLEMENTAL CLAIM
Additional to the Scope of Repairs

Dated _____

INSURED _____

ADDRESS _____

CITY STATE ZIP _____

H/PH _____

B/PH _____

INSURANCE CO. _____

POLICY # _____

CLAIM # _____

DATE OF LOSS _____

TYPE OF LOSS _____

AREA NAME   AREA DIMENSIONS   PG____OF____

DESCRIPTION	#/U	U/M	PPU	COST

LEGEND

Days-No. of Days	AMP-Amperes	AVG-Average	BINS-No. of Bins	CF-Cubic Feet	CFDAY-Cost/CF/Day	CY-Cubic Yards	D-Depth
LI-Lineal Inch	EA-Each Unit	EST-Estimated Amount	H-Height	HRS-No. of Hours	L-Long	LDS-No. of Loads	LF-Lineal Feet
SFF-Sq Foot of Floor	L/M-Labor& Materials	M/C-Minimum Charge	PR-Pair	PPU-Price per Unit	R&R-Remove/Replace/Reset	S/C-Service Charge	SF-Square Feet
SYW-Sq Yd Walls	SFC-Sq Foot Ceiling	SFW-Sq Foot of Walls	SQ-Square of Roofing	SY-Square Yard	SYC-Sq Yd Ceiling	SYF-Sq Yd Floor	SYL-Sq Yd Linoleum
	T&G-Tongue& Groove	TK/D-Truck Loads per Day	U/M-Unit of Measure	V-Volts	W-Wide	w/-With	#/U-No. of Units

ADDITIONAL /CHANGE WORK AUTHORIZATION

OWNER'S NAME	DATE
ADDRESS	JOB LOCATION
EXISTING CONTRACT DATE	PHONE

YOU ARE HEREBY AUTHORIZED TO PERFORM THE FOLLOWING SPECIFICALLY DESCRIBED ADDITIONAL OR CHANGED WORK:

ADDITIONAL CHARGE FOR ABOVE WORK IS: $ _____

PAYMENT WILL BE MADE AS FOLLOWS:

ABOVE ADDITIONAL WORK TO BE PERFORMED UNDER SAME CONDITIONS AS
SPECIFIED IN ORIGINAL CONTRACT UNLESS OTHERWISE STIPULATED.

WE HEREBY AGREE TO FURNISH LABOR AND MATERIALS-COMPLETE IN ACCORDANCE
WITH THE ABOVE SPECIFICATIONS, AT ABOVE STATED PRICE.

OWNER SIGNATURE   DATE   CONTRACTOR SIGNATURE   DATE

THIS IS CHANGE ORDER NO.

NOTE: THIS REVISION BECOMES PART OF AND IN ACCORDANCE WITH EXISTING WORK AUTHORIZATION OR CONTRACT.

See Chapter 14 for a general explanation of this form

CONDITIONAL WAIVER AND RELEASE UPON PROGRESS PAYMENT

Upon receipt by the undersigned of a check from _____ in the sum of _____ payable to _____ and when the check has been properly endorsed and has been paid by the bank upon which it is drawn, this document shall become effective to release any mechanic's lien stop notice or bondright the undersigned has on the job of _____located at _____ _____ _____to the following extent. This release covers a progress payment for labor, services, equipment, or material furnished to _____through _____ only and does not cover any retentions retained before or after the release date; extras furnished before the release date for which payment has not been received; extras or items furnished after the release date. Rights based upon work performed or items furnished under a written change order which has been fully executed by the parties prior to the release date are covered by this release unless specifically reserved by the claimant in this release. This release of any mechanic's lien, stop notice, or bondright shall not otherwise affect the contract rights, including rights between parties to the contract based upon a recission, abandonment, or breach of the contract, or the right of the undersigned to recover compensation for furnished labor, services, equipment, or material covered by this release if that furnished labor, services, equipment, or material was not compensated by the progress payment. Before any recipient of this document relies on it, said party should verify evidence of payment to the undersigned.

Dated: _____   _____

                                            By_____

THE UNDERSIGNED HAVE PERFORMED LABOR FOR WAGES ON THE PROJECT DESCRIBED ON FACE OF FORM AND HAVE BEEN PAID IN FULL TO DATE

_____   _____
(Signature of Individual Performing Labor for Wages) (Date)   (Signature of Individual Performing Labor for Wages) (Date)

_____   _____
(Signature of Individual Performing Labor for Wages) (Date)   (Signature of Individual Performing Labor for Wages) (Date)

_____   _____
(Signature of Individual Performing Labor for Wages) (Date)   (Signature of Individual Performing Labor for Wages) (Date)

_____   _____
(Signature of Individual Performing Labor for Wages) (Date)   (Signature of Individual Performing Labor for Wages) (Date)

_____   _____
(Signature of Individual Performing Labor for Wages) (Date)   (Signature of Individual Performing Labor for Wages) (Date)

See Chapter 14 for a general explanation of this form

UNCONDITIONAL WAIVER AND RELEASE UPON PROGRESS PAYMENT

The undersigned has been paid and has received a progress payment in the sum of $_____ for labor, services, equipment,
(Amount of Check)

or material furnished to_____ located at _____
(Owner)   (Job Address)

and does hereby release any mechanic's lien, stop notice, or bondright that the undersigned has on the above referenced job to the following extent. This release covers a progress payment for labor, services, equipment, or materials furnished to

_____ through _____ only and does not cover any retentions retained before or
(Your Customer)   (Date)

after the release date; extras furnished before the release date for which payment has not been received; extras or items furnished after the release date. Rights based upon work performed or items furnished under a written change order which has been fully executed by the parties prior to the release date are covered by this release unless specifically reserved by the claimant in this release. This release of any mechanic's lien, stop notice, or bondright shall not otherwise affect the contract rights, including rights between parties to the contract based upon a recision, abandonment, or breach of contract, or the right of the undersigned to recover compensation for furnished labor, services, equipment, or material covered by this release if that furnished labor, services equipment, or material was not compensated by the progress payment.

Dated: _____

_____
(Company Name)

By_____
(Title)

NOTICE TO PERSONS SIGNING THIS WAIVER: THIS DOCUMENT WAIVES RIGHTS UNCONDITIONALLY AND STATES THAT YOU HAVE BEEN PAID FOR GIVING UP THOSE RIGHTS. THIS DOCUMENT IS ENFORCEABLE AGAINST YOU IF YOU SIGN IT, EVEN IF YOU HAVE NOT BEEN PAID. IF YOU HAVE NOT BEEN PAID, USE A CONDITIONAL RELEASE FORM.

THE UNDERSIGNED HAVE PERFORMED LABOR FOR WAGES ON THE PROJECT DESCRIBED ON FACE OF FORM AND HAVE BEEN PAID IN FULL TO DATE

_____
(Signature of Individual Performing Labor for Wages) (Date)

_____
(Signature of Individual Performing Labor for Wages) (Date)

_____
(Signature of Individual Performing Labor for Wages) (Date)

_____
(Signature of Individual Performing Labor for Wages) (Date)

_____
(Signature of Individual Performing Labor for Wages) (Date)

_____
(Signature of Individual Performing Labor for Wages) (Date)

_____
(Signature of Individual Performing Labor for Wages) (Date)

_____
(Signature of Individual Performing Labor for Wages) (Date)

See Chapter 14 for a general explanation of this form

UNCONDITIONAL WAIVER AND RELEASE UPON FINAL PAYMENT

The undersigned has been paid in full for all labor, services, equipment or material furnished to _____
(Homeowner Name)

at the address of _____ and does hereby waive and release any mechanic's lien, stop notice, or
(Address)

any bondright against a labor and material bond on the job, except for disputed claims for extra work in the amount of $_____.

Dated: _____

_____
(Company Name)

By _____
(Title)

NOTICE TO PERSONS SIGNING THIS WAIVER: THIS DOCUMENT WAIVES RIGHTS UNCONDITIONALLY AND STATES THAT YOU HAVE BEEN PAID FOR GIVING UP THOSE RIGHTS. THIS DOCUMENT IS ENFORCEABLE AGAINST YOU IF YOU SIGN IT, EVEN IF YOU HAVE NOT BEEN PAID. IF YOU HAVE NOT BEEN PAID, USE A CONDITIONAL RELEASE FORM.

THE UNDERSIGNED HAVE PERFORMED LABOR FOR WAGES ON THE PROJECT DESCRIBED ON FACE OF FORM AND HAVE BEEN PAID IN FULL TO DATE

_____
(Signature of Individual Performing Labor for Wages)   (Date)

_____
(Signature of Individual Performing Labor for Wages)   (Date)

_____
(Signature of Individual Performing Labor for Wages)   (Date)

_____
(Signature of Individual Performing Labor for Wages)   (Date)

_____
(Signature of Individual Performing Labor for Wages)   (Date)

_____
(Signature of Individual Performing Labor for Wages)   (Date)

_____
(Signature of Individual Performing Labor for Wages)   (Date)

_____
(Signature of Individual Performing Labor for Wages)   (Date)

_____
(Signature of Individual Performing Labor for Wages)   (Date)

_____
(Signature of Individual Performing Labor for Wages)   (Date)

RESTORATION
SMALL LITTLE DETAILS (SLD)
LIST

Date _____

	DESCRIPTION OF ITEM TO BE CORRECTED	DATE GIVEN TO CONTRACTOR	DATE CORRECTED	✔
1				
2				
3				
4				
5				
6				
7				
8				
9				
10				
11				
12				
13				
14				
15				
16				
17				
18				
19				
20				
21				
22				
23				
24				
25				
26				
27				

NOTES

NOTES